It's a Family Affair

A Teen Guide to Parents and How to Survive Them

By Youth Communication

Edited by Al Desetta

It's a Family Affair

EXECUTIVE EDITORS
Keith Hefner and Laura Longhine

CONTRIBUTING EDITORS
Hope Vanderberg, Clarence Haynes, Andrea Estepa, Philip Kay, Rachel Blustain, Marie Glancy, Laura Longhine, and Alexandra Ringe

LAYOUT & DESIGN
Efrain Reyes, Jr. and Jeff Faerber

COVER ART
Odessa Straub / YC Art Dept.

Copyright © 2009 by Youth Communication®

All rights reserved under International and Pan-American Copyright Conventions. Unless otherwise noted, no part of this book may be reproduced, stored in a retrieval system, or transmitted in any form or by any means, electronic, mechanical, photocopying, recording, or otherwise, without express written permission of the publisher, except for brief quotations or critical reviews.

For reprint information, please contact Youth Communication.

ISBN 978-1-933939-74-2

Second, Expanded Edition

Printed in the United States of America

Youth Communication®
New York, NY
www.youthcomm.org

Table of Contents

The Parent Trap, *Lucas Mann* 11
    Lucas is here to tell the truth: there is no Santa Claus, puppies die, and parents don't trust their kids when they're out of sight.

Finding Our Way Home, *Janelle Allen* 16
    When Janelle returns to her mother from foster care, they have to rebuild their relationship.

Meeting the Invisible Man, *Athena Karoutsos* 22
    At age 15, Athena visits her long-absent father in Greece.

Far From the Mom I Love, *Anonymous* 29
    When the writer immigrates to the U.S. she has to leave her mother behind.

At Home Away From Home, *Odé Manderson* 35
    Ode's longs to escape his mother's demands.

Prisoner In My Own House, *Anonymous* 41
    The writer's strict parents crack down when they discover she's been disobeying them to date boys.

She'll Always Be My Mother, *Wunika Hicks* 45
    Wunika is abused and neglected by her mother, but still feels connected to her.

Contents

Mom, Dad, I Have Something to Tell You, *Jose M. Jimenez* 52
> Jose fears telling his parents he is gay.

Not Quite a Family, *Anonymous* 57
> The writer deals with a difficult stepfather.

My Father: I Want to be Everything He's Not, *Troy Shawn Welcome* 64
> Troy wants to be close to his father, but keeps getting let down.

My Mother Almost Didn't Come Home, *Nicolle Lewis* 70
> When Nicolle's mother suffers a stroke, Nicolle is gripped by the fear of losing her.

He's Not My Grandpa! *Megan Cohen* 75
> Megan has much older parents than her peers.

Trapped by Mom's Rules, *Anonymous* 80
> The writer feels overwhelmed by her overprotective mother.

My Parents Gave Me Everything—Except Themselves, *Lily Mai* 86
> Lily feels neglected by her hardworking immigrant parents, until she travels to China and sees the poverty they escaped by coming to America.

Contents

Her Shining Star?, *T. Garrido* 91
  The writer and her mother work through a devastating fight.

Communication: How to Get It Started, *Anonymous* 98
  A therapist and a social worker give teens advice on how to talk to their parents.

FICTION SPECIAL: Lost and Found, *Anne Schraff* 101

Teens: How to Get More Out of This Book 110

How to Use This Book in Staff Training 111

Teachers and Staff: How to Use This Book In Groups 112

Credits 114

About Youth Communication 115

About the Editors 118

More Helpful Books from Youth Communication 120

Introduction

Most teens value close relations with their parents. That theme unites the 16 true stories in It's a Family Affair. Whether they feel loved and respected, or misunderstood and abandoned, these young authors write with honesty and insight about the impact their parents have had on their lives.

Not surprisingly, many stories deal with the conflicts that result from having strict and overprotective parents. "I'm sorry to be the one to say this," writes Lucas Mann, "but there is no Santa Claus, puppies die, and parents don't trust." Lucas goes on to describe the various interrogation styles parents use when they suspect their teens of wrongdoing.

The mother of one writer calls "every hour on the hour" to check up on her, even though she's already 18. The writer understands her mother's concerns, since they live in a dangerous neighborhood, but she rebels against the suffocating rules by doing exactly what her mother doesn't want her to do—dating boys. Ode Manderson longs to escape his nagging mother by going to college. "At 17, I want to do what I want and make my own choices," he writes. "My mom feels differently."

Other writers describe the pain of having unresolved conflicts with neglectful or absent parents. Athena Karoutsos and Troy Shawn Welcome both have to come to terms with the realization that their on-again, off-again fathers may never be able to give them the support and closeness they're longing for.

Wunika Hicks suffers terrible abuse from her mother, and is left home for days at a time with only her infant brother's baby food to eat. Yet she is inextricably bound to her mom: "I didn't want my mother to go, just her attitude. I knew if she went away, I'd have nothing. She was a part of me and vice versa, regardless of all the bad things."

When Lily Mai visits her mother's poverty-stricken hometown in China, she realizes that her parents spend so much time working because they want her to have an easier life. But she still longs to have a close and affectionate relationship with them. "I would've given up the big house and TV and gone back to live in Chinatown if I could have had my parents around," she writes.

Fortunately, many of the writers and their parents have found ways to work through their difficulties or reconnect.

In "Finding Our Way Home," Janelle Allen grows distant from her mother after going into foster care, and is angry when she returns home. But Janelle's mother takes them to family therapy, where they both learn how to listen to and trust each other.

When Tashiana Garrido's mother reads her diary and finds out about her boyfriends, the two don't talk for months. But then they open up communication, the mother relaxes certain rules, and the two build a healthier, stronger relationship.

And in "Far From the Mom I Love," the author feels a renewed appreciation for her mother, who remains behind in Kenya when the writer joins her father in New York. "Suddenly I felt incomplete, like half of me had died," she writes. "We were broke back in Kenya and sometimes I had only one meal a day, but I had my mom."

In the following stories, names and/or identifying details have been changed: *Far From the Mom I Love, Prisoner In My Own House, Not Quite a Family, Mom's Rules Make Me Feel Trapped*, and *Her Shining Star?*

The Parent Trap

By Lucas Mann

It's 1 a.m., and I'm walking home from playing pool. I'm not clear about when I was supposed to be home, because my parents have decided to "test the waters" and see if I'm responsible enough to call them and work out when I should come home.

Of course, I haven't called. And the fact that I've received three voice mails from home in the past hour doesn't bode well for me. I approach my house and come to a sickening realization: I can't find my keys. I empty every cargo pocket I have and move on to my backpack.

At 1:10, I realize my keys are on the kitchen counter where I'd left them the night before. Terrified, I ring the doorbell. In a few moments, my bleary-eyed mother opens the door.

"Why didn't you pick up the phone?" she asks.

"There was loud music, Mom."

"Loud music, huh? Where were you?"

"At the pool place."
"Drinking?"
"No."
"Drugs?"
"No."
"At least I don't have to worry about you getting some girl pregnant."
"Thanks, Mom."

Just about every teen I know has dealt with a similar situation. Maybe they were smart enough to remember their keys, but there's still a bleary-eyed parent hiding in the shadows by the doorway.

You're probably late. You probably forgot to call. You've tickled their nose with a hint of something forbidden. People say hounds can smell better than anything. They're wrong. Parents have the best sense of smell in the animal kingdom. Smart hunters would take their moms with them.

Some may read this and object. "My parents aren't like that. My parents trust me." No, they don't. It's not in a parent's make-up to trust.

Maybe your parents trust you more than most parents, maybe they try to push their suspicions down, but they don't really trust you. I'm sorry to be the one to say this, but there is no Santa Claus, puppies die, and parents don't trust.

Everyone's parents have their own way to interrogate their kids. The Barbara Walters have a constant barrage of questions: "Where were you? Why are you late? Who were you with? What did I hear in the background when I called you?"

Some parents just scream. We'll call them the Scream Machines. They wake up your siblings, your pets, your neighbors, and nearby pigeon roosts.

"My dad yells so much that he forgets what he's yelling about, and just goes to bed," said my friend Allie, an experienced night owl.

Many kids, though, have quiet parents. They wait with sinister smiles, armed with mind games, waiting for slip-ups. I call them the Dr. Evils because they always have a diabolical plot.

They observe everything. One anonymous parent called her son (my friend) and heard loud music and voices in the background. He claimed to be at a movie. This sly parent had heard about underage dance parties, though, and had suspicions.

She sat at home, waiting, plotting, waiting, plotting. She remembered the stamps that they put on hands at clubs sometimes. I can only imagine the devious smile that crossed her face.

I'm sorry to say this, but there is no Santa Claus, puppies die, and parents don't trust.

The poor son came home. She asked him how the movie was. He unwittingly dug his own grave, making up details about a movie they both knew he hadn't seen. She inspected his hands. Sure enough, a bright green star adorned his left hand. Caught, green handed.

Some Dr. Evils like to drag it out. I once stayed at a friend's house (we'll call him Bob) and we came home at a truly ungodly hour. It's tricky. His parents don't set a curfew for him, but still assume he's out doing something illegal if he comes home late.

I was braced for quite a yelling, but the door opened to a bright smile and a "Hi, boys." Amazed, we hurried off to bed. How naïve we were.

The next morning, Mary Poppins morphed into the Wicked Witch of the West. Clearly, she had prepared for this, studied through the night, dreamt of this moment. She grilled her son like a piece of steak. "So, were you in late last night because you were drinking?" she said, with a perfectly pleasant smile.

"No, Mom."

"Then why did you smell like it?"

"Maybe you imagined it."

"No, I'm pretty sure."

"Fine. I met a few people who'd been drinking and they

smelled strong. I guess it rubbed off."

"Oh, so now you hang out with the kind of people who drink?"

"No, Mom…" Bob ran to his room, humiliated.

Bob's mother settled back into her nice normal self and resumed breakfast with me and Bob's younger brother.

Nice parents, who pretend to trust, might just be the worst of all. They're the 007s. My own folks fit this category. "We understand, dear. We trust you," they purr. "And you can tell us if you're doing something wrong. We won't be mad. We'll talk about it. Just don't lie."

> **We should wait until we're in weekly therapy and our parents have mellowed before we try to understand them.**

This past summer they took away my curfew, saying they trusted me to call and work out a reasonable time with them on the spot. They trust me to be where I say I am. They trust me not to drink or do drugs. They love me.

But wait! It's a trap! They act so nice that I feel guilt. Lots of guilt. I feel terrible for even thinking about doing something wrong. There's a battle raging between my conscience and my parents' expectations, and I haven't even done anything.

Of course, I'm not writing this with pure objectivity. When parents are suspicious, sometimes we give them reason. If we come home late, if we get caught lying about where we were, if we smell like beer—we have it coming.

Plus, if parents weren't the way they were, many of us wouldn't make it past 18 with our sanity and health intact. And, in turn, if teens didn't act the way we do, parents would be… well, actually, they'd be a lot happier.

Still, it is frustrating. We're frustrated when we get constantly questioned and our parents are frustrated to be up at midnight, wondering if we're alive. Parents are sometimes too overprotective and teens are prone to take a foot if you give us an inch. And the standard teenage one-word response is enough to make parents suspicious, even if we're not guilty.

I think that it's important for both parents and teens to realize that we won't see eye to eye. We teens should wait until our 20s, when we're in weekly therapy and our parents have mellowed, before we try to understand them.

The main key is to not start a war now. Parents are going to be parents, no matter what. If you can smile about something instead of having a confrontation about it every weekend, I say go for it.

Humor's also an option, and it's helped me have a better relationship with my parents than anybody I know. When asked where I am, I say: "The crack house."

"OK," my dad answers. "Just make sure you're not driving home."

Truthfully, we teens have limited options when it comes to dealing with parents because of one annoying fact: they have tons of power and we don't. Coming home drunk or breaking curfew just gives them fuel.

If you're a kid who follows the rules, you always have the option of pointing out: "Hey, I could be a lot worse." Even this will probably be ineffective, though. So the best thing to do is simply close your eyes and dream of that light at the end of the tunnel: turning 18.

One day, you'll be free.

Lucas was 16 when he wrote this story.
He graduated from college and works in publishing.

Finding Our Way Home

By Janelle Allen

When I was young, life with my mother was good. I used to love going to her old job, playing with whatever I could play with and watching her at work. I remember playing little hand games with her like "thumb war" and "boom-boom clap-clap." I remember going to day care and not wanting her to leave me, because I just wanted her to stay with me all day long. No matter how I was feeling, I was always glad to see my mom because she always made me feel good.

But as I got a little older, it seemed like my mom was always stressed out. My brother was getting into trouble at school and his teachers would call her almost every day. My mother became very depressed and tired of having to deal with the same problems all the time.

It wasn't hard to notice because she would complain about

whatever made her angry and upset—her job, her kids, or the landlord who wasn't doing his job fixing up the apartment. My mother wasn't happy anymore. She always looked sad, like a big cloud was over her shoulder that could rain on her any day.

I didn't understand why she was feeling this way or why she was starting to hate her life so much. All I remember is that things were not good and that I felt like my life would probably never be the same.

I always knew she loved us, but she just had a lot of problems that brought her spirit down. She was having so many problems with my brother's school, and having to go pick him up all the time, that she quit her job. My dad wasn't around, and there is only so much a person can handle. My mother didn't stop doing her duties as a parent, but she basically didn't seem to care anymore about having fun with us and making us laugh.

As the days went on, my mom started getting worse. She'd tell us that she was not doing her best with us and not giving us enough. She thought we needed a better life than what we had and the only person she felt could give that to us was my aunt Gina, her closest sister.

One day a worker from child welfare showed up. She had dark skin and hair and she always wore black. My mother didn't like her at all. Later, I found out that a counselor at my brother's school had called child welfare after my mother said she was fed up and couldn't take it anymore.

Even though my mom had been talking about us going to live with Aunt Gina, I wasn't prepared for the social worker to take us away. The day we left, my mother wasn't around, and I had no clue what was going on. I was just scared and wanted this whole thing to be over.

I remember being put in a car that was very uncomfortable. It was a long drive, and I thought that when we came out of the car I would be in front of my aunt's building. That's where I wanted to be. But I was in front of someone else's building.

Luckily, the foster mother was nice, and my brother and I stayed at her home for about a month with no problems. I would get phone calls from my mother from time to time. She'd ask me how I was doing, tell me how much she missed me and how she couldn't wait to see me.

I missed my mom a lot, too. I really wondered what she was doing and where she was and what exactly had happened to her that day we got taken away. But I never asked her any of those questions.

> *My mother said she wasn't going to give up on us again; she was going to find some way to solve this problem. And she did.*

After a month, we moved to my aunt's house. Life with my aunt was great. I started going to a new Catholic school and I loved it. My aunt worked there and everyone knew her name.

My mother would call sometimes and ask me if I wanted to see her and come home. Of course I said yes, but I really didn't mean it at all. I enjoyed being at my aunt's and wanted to stay there forever. I just didn't want to tell my mom that and make her feel bad.

The first time I went to visit my mother I thought I would be happy to see her, but it was kind of weird. I acted like everything was fine, but I didn't really feel comfortable talking to my own mother and I wasn't sure why. My mom was so happy to see us and she couldn't stop smiling. We stayed for a little while, then hugged each other and said our good-byes and that was it.

My mother got the chance to visit us on holidays and birthdays, which was great, but I felt more distant toward her, like I didn't want to see her at all. I knew it wasn't right, but that's how I felt at the time. I didn't show it or tell anyone. I just left it alone.

After three years at my aunt's house she told us it was time for us to leave. I couldn't accept the fact that I was going to be coming home to my mother and living in the life I'd once left behind. Going back to my past was a slap in the face. I had my life here—my friends, my school and everything else—and now I had to leave it. This hurt me so much.

It was very hard readjusting to my mother and my new life. My mother seemed so happy to finally have us back. She'd made many changes in her life while my brother and I were gone. I think one of the biggest changes she made was with her anger.

My mother used to get so angry whenever someone would give her attitude. She would yell at the top of her lungs while cussing them out. But since we'd left it seemed like she'd learned how to control that. She seemed calmer, like she was at peace with herself.

Another change was my mom's new boyfriend. When I met him I didn't like him at all. I knew it was wrong to judge a book by its cover, but there was just something about him that convinced me not to trust him.

My mother liked him a lot, though, I could tell, and so did my brother. I felt like an outcast because I was the only one who didn't. My mother noticed and talked to me about it, but I just didn't care. I started not to care about a lot of things that my mother told me to do or not do.

I didn't listen to her or give her any respect. I started talking back and arguing with her all the time. I guess since I'd been gone for a while I thought the only person I should be listening to was my aunt. I knew my mother had the right to give me rules, but I just felt like, "Why should I listen to them?"

My mother didn't know what to do with my brother and me because we were both being so disrespectful toward her all the time. She said she wasn't going to give up on us again; she was going to find some way to solve this problem. And she did.

She took all of us to family counseling, which I thought was stupid at first. I didn't think it would work.

When we got to our first session I was nervous. I hated being there and I just wanted to leave and go home, but I couldn't. So I sat there and listened to my mother talk to the therapist. Everything she was saying was true. My mom seemed not at all uncomfortable telling her business, but I was. I didn't know the therapist at all and I really didn't feel like telling her anything.

But each day we went there I felt more comfortable and open. The therapist was really nice and we each got a chance to say what we were feeling out loud to one another. It took me a while, but once I got to talking I couldn't stop. I told the therapist how I was feeling, the problems I was having with my mom and everything else about myself. We talked for hours, but I always felt like we didn't really have enough time.

As the years went by I started noticing a change in myself as well as my mother. We were getting along much better and talking to each other. And it didn't hurt that she'd gotten rid of that boyfriend.

Being able to talk out our problems without yelling at one another made a big difference in our lives.

In therapy, my mother was getting a better understanding of how my brother and I felt and I got a better understanding of how she felt. Being able to talk out our problems without yelling at one another made a big difference in our lives. We started really listening to each other and I felt that we were gaining back the bond we once had.

It's been seven years now since I came home, and my mother and I have a fun relationship. We play around with one another all the time, making jokes and laughing so loud and hard at whatever we think is funny. I love my mother a lot and I feel like the older I'm getting the more I'm starting to appreciate her (even though she doesn't think that).

I love talking to her and I feel she understands me in so many ways, although she still has doubts about me because I don't tell her every little thing. I don't feel comfortable telling her every detail of my social life, but I do feel like I have a better connection with her than I did before.

My mother is a strong woman who has dealt with a lot in her life and somehow gotten out of it. I see her as a good person to look up to, even though she doesn't think she is. She tells me all the time that she's made so many mistakes in her life and that I should learn from them.

My mom thinks I don't listen to her when she tells me things, but I am listening in my own little way. I know when I get older I'll look back and know exactly what she meant. I don't always show my appreciation, but I know I'm lucky to have a mother like her.

In the past I felt like I would never be able to forgive my mother for putting me through all this. But now that that I'm older I feel like I can accept the fact that it happened and move on with my life, one day at a time.

Janelle was 17 when she wrote this story.

Meeting the Invisible Man

By Athena Karoutsos

The last time I saw my father was three years ago, when I was 15. My mom and I had spent the summer in Greece, where he lives. I was about to go back to America and we were sitting in his car, just him and me.

I looked out the window. It was black outside and the dust from the road flew up in the air, making the darkness seem like it was sparkling. I thought of how close my father and I had become that summer. We'd spent almost every day together sitting in cafes drinking European lemonade, going to see other towns and visiting relatives.

I didn't want to go back to New York and let it be like it had been before. I hadn't seen my father for six years before that summer and this was the first time we'd really spent any time together.

My father could tell I was anxious. "Don't worry. I promise things will change," he said in Greek. "We'll call each other now. If you ever need anything, just tell me and I'll send it to you."

I stayed silent. His words seemed too good to be true. "Why should things change now?" I thought to myself. Still, I wanted to believe him.

As a little kid, I hated Father's Day. When the teacher made us draw cards for our fathers and all the other kids fought over the markers, glitter and colored paper, I always felt empty inside.

One year when I was about 6, I watched the other kids scribble on the bright paper and felt embarrassed because I had nothing to do. When the teacher asked me why I wasn't joining in, I had to tell her I didn't have a father. She asked me if I knew anyone else who was a father and told me to make a card for them. I made a card for my uncle.

Before that I had never thought of my father. I knew everyone had one but I didn't know exactly what a father was. But now I began to wonder, if everyone else had a father, why didn't I? A few months after the card-making incident I asked my mom about him.

She told me how she'd gone to visit her family in Greece one summer. When she was on the boat going to the island she's from, Ikaria, she saw my father looking at her. Soon after that they fell in love.

My mom got pregnant with me, and my father told her to live in his apartment while he was away. (He's a first mechanic on boats so he spends half the year at sea.) But my mother didn't want to stay there alone and she needed to come back to America to take care of her mother, who was sick. Besides, she wanted me to be born in New York so I would be a U.S. citizen. So after a few months she went home to New York.

When I was born, my mother called my father and told him I was a girl, but he didn't seem happy. She was so upset that when the hospital staff asked for my father's name for my birth certificate, she left it blank.

He'd never come to see me, but my mom reminded me that I'd met my father once, two years before, when I was 4. She showed me some pictures of us together in his apartment in Athens (the largest city and capital of Greece).

There was one picture of me watching him shave and another of him reading to me while I held a doll. I suddenly remembered how I had left the doll there. I missed the doll and didn't think of anything else. My father seemed like a stranger to me.

Most of the time, I didn't feel anything was missing from my life. My mother gave me whatever I needed and tried her best to give me what I wanted. And I had the rest of my family, too. My aunt and uncle threw me big birthday parties and let me bring my friends to their house in Long Island for the weekend. They bought me toys and gave me ballet lessons. My other uncle took me shopping and even gave me spending money, since my mom often couldn't.

He was so close to me but at the same time so unreachable, like he'd always been.

I saw my father again briefly when I was 8 and my mom took me to Greece, but all I remember was pulling my hand away when he tried to hold it and meeting his new wife. After that I didn't see him until we went to Greece again, the summer I turned 15.

By this time I had several friends whose parents weren't together. But their fathers called them and saw them as often as they could, even if they lived in other countries. I never even got one phone call.

For the first time, I wanted to see my father. I wanted to ask him, "Why?" I knew half of myself but I didn't know the other half. I was growing up and I wanted to know myself as a whole. So when my mom told me he was going to be in Ikaria that summer and he wanted to see me, I was glad, though nervous.

But once we got to Greece, I felt unsure if I was ready to see him. I was filled with the same uncertainty that I feel when I think about death, that there's no way to know what it's going to be like until it happens.

I watched my father a few times before I met him. The first time, my mom and I were eating on the balcony of a café in Ikaria and my father and his wife passed by down below us. My mom pointed him out to me. Another time I was in a taxi and I passed by him sitting at his sister's restaurant. Each time I couldn't believe it was him. He was so close to me but at the same time so unreachable, like he'd always been.

After a few days, I decided I had to meet him if I was ever going to get any answers. My mother, who wanted me to have a relationship with him as much as I did, was relieved. She planned for me to meet him at my aunt's restaurant that night.

Of course he was late. I sat in the restaurant waiting and felt too much all at once—sadness, fear and hope. When I saw him come in, I felt my heart in my throat. I couldn't move.

He looked nothing like he had in the few photographs I had of him. Age had caught up with him. He'd grown a round belly. His hair was thin and straight, not curly and thick like in the photos. When he smiled, his teeth were yellow and chipped.

He came over to hug me but I just stood there and wouldn't hug him back. So he shook my hand. My father was shaking and his eyes were wet. I had always thought of him as emotionless. I hadn't thought he might be as nervous about our meeting as I was.

Everyone was staring at us—his wife, my mother, my cousins, my aunt and uncle. He told me to sit down and got me a Sprite. I couldn't speak or drink. I couldn't even feel the cold glass in my hand. Then he asked me to go for a ride in his car so we could be alone to talk.

When we were in the car I wanted to say so many things. He

just asked me how I was, how my mom was and how my aunt and uncles were doing. Then I finally burst out, "Why don't you ever call or write to me?"

He sat, thinking. Finally he stuttered, "I tried calling once. Did you change your number? I lost your address."

What shocked me most was how lame his answer was. "Couldn't he at least have had the decency to make up a good excuse?" I thought.

My thoughts raced. "I'm his only child. I don't care if he willingly or unwillingly made me. I am a part of him. How could he abandon a part of him? How could he not even care to know how I was all these years? What if I was suffering? What if I was dead? He wouldn't have known. Did he even care?" I thought. But I said nothing because it was hard enough asking the first question.

We drove back in silence. It hit me that maybe he had no idea how badly he was treating me and if I was ever going to have a relationship with my father I'd have to be the one to do something. Even though I thought he didn't deserve forgiveness, I knew it was the only way for things to change. So inside of me I forgave him.

I ended up having a wonderful summer. I got to spend time with him, which was all that mattered to me. He'd try to buy me things, but I didn't want his money. I just wanted his time. I wanted to know I was worth my father's time.

One day we drove to a town on the other side of the island. We sat down at a restaurant and ordered something to eat. "Do you want some lemonade?" my father struggled to ask in English. His terrible accent was endearing and I laughed. "Why are you laughing? Is it funny how I said that?" he said in Greek, smiling.

"No," I lied, as I tried to control my laughter. Then the food came. We didn't talk but the silence had become more comfortable.

Though I saw him nearly every day that summer, we never really talked. I learned only a few things about my father, and one was how similar he was to me when it came to expressing emotions out loud. I could tell how my father kept it all inside and I saw regret in his eyes.

But even though there was silence between us, I liked being near my father. It made me feel safe to know that if anything were to happen he was there to protect me, like a father should. I spent every moment I could with him. I even called him "Father," and when I did he would smile. I knew I made my father happy. I felt complete.

I wanted to know I was worth my father's time.

The summer passed by quickly and soon it was time to leave. We sat in his car that one last time and he made his promise—his lie. As soon as I came back to New York I went out in the pouring rain to buy a calling card because I missed my father.

When I called there was that silence between us again. He asked if I was all right and if I needed anything, and then we couldn't think of anything else to say. After that phone call the days went by and he never called. I waited for a letter and it never came.

It's been three years now and I haven't heard from him. Things are just like they were before that visit. Except in a sense it's worse now because I know what I'm missing.

I don't think my father is someone anyone can have any kind of relationship with. He doesn't talk to his own mother and he has gotten divorced from his wife. I think his mind is like a child's and he doesn't know right from wrong. He doesn't realize all the people he's hurting. I feel sorry for him but I'm tired of trying and I don't think I'll try again. It's not worth the pain.

Despite all this, I'm not angry at myself for trusting him. In fact, I still do trust him. There are many ways to trust someone and I trust that though he won't be there for me, he does love me.

I wouldn't take back that summer because it gave me good memories of my father. And even though I don't expect it, I will never stop waiting for him to call.

Athena was 17 when she wrote this story. She graduated high school and attended the City College of New York.

Far From the Mom I Love

By Anonymous

As a child I lived in Kenya, in Africa, with my family. Our lives were great up until I turned 5. Then everything changed.

My father went to America, and my mother, three siblings, and I had to move out of our house since it belonged to the company he worked for. We couldn't afford an apartment and had to live in a church for about three years. My mother's job didn't pay much and my father wasn't sending us any money, so things were very hard.

But I didn't really know my family was poor until I was about 10, because my mom never acted the way I thought poor people did. I went to a private school with rich people. My mom took us to expensive restaurants sometimes and tried her best to get everything we wanted. She even threw my little brother and me the biggest birthday party my school had ever seen, and everyone thought we were rich.

On Christmas and Easter we'd buy cows, sheep, and chickens. My brothers would kill the animals, and my sister and mom would make the biggest meals ever. Christmas was always the best because we'd all get together to pray, laugh, and eat.

My mother always made things seem easy, so I didn't realize for a long time how much she sacrificed for my siblings and me. But it became clear one day when I was in 4th grade. I was getting ready for school and my mom looked worried, so I asked her what was wrong.

"Nothing," she said. "Go get ready or you'll be late."

I knew she was lying, so I pushed harder and asked her over and over again. She got quiet for a while and then said, "I don't have enough money to get me to work and you to school."

Now that she wasn't with me, I felt like there was no one to be proud of me.

I knew that my mom missing one day of work meant less money for us. "I could miss school, we're not doing anything today," I said. I knew she was going to say no, but I said it anyway.

"No! What did I tell you about going to school every day? I'll give the money to you and figure out a way to get to work. Don't worry, everything is going to be OK."

I figured that she would borrow money from one of her friends, so I took the money and left for school. I was having a good day until my best friend told me she had seen my mom while she was on her way to school. My friend lived about three blocks away from where my mom worked, so that meant my mom had walked all the way from our house to her job. It took about 35 minutes to get there by cab, so walking must have taken her hours.

I was so mad that I went into the school bathroom and prayed to God to forgive my mom for any sin she ever committed to deserve such struggles. I wanted to help her so badly but I didn't know how. I cried so hard that I had a headache at the end of school.

I loved my mom for sacrificing herself for my siblings and me. I felt she understood me like no one else did, and she inspired me to be my best. When she gave me the money to go to school that day, it was because she wanted me to do well and become a doctor.

But I was also mad that she put her kids first no matter what. Sometimes we didn't have enough food, and she'd refuse to eat so we'd have enough. One year she took my sister and me shopping for Christmas and she bought us many expensive clothes she couldn't afford. She told the owner of the store—her friend since high school—that she was expecting a great amount of money from one of my uncles in America and she'd pay for the clothes when she got it.

But she couldn't pay the lady back because she never got the money, and she had to go to jail for it. She told me she was going to be working in the police station for a while, and I believed her. It wasn't until a year later that I learned the truth from my sister.

Every human has a breaking point, but I felt that my mother didn't. If she got into an argument with someone, she would try to make peace with the person to set a good example for us, because she believes you should never face evil with more evil.

Seeing her suffer because of this goodness made me want to act the opposite way. I became defensive and would talk back to anyone who started anything with me. Sometimes I overreacted to little things because I didn't want to seem weak.

And until I left my country, I took my mother's love for granted because I thought she was always going to be there. Then, when I was 11, I got a phone call from one of my uncles on my father's side of the family. He said my brothers and I were going to live with my father in America.

I was so used to moving around that I didn't think much about it, or about the fact that my mom wasn't coming with us.

When I was saying my good-byes, nobody told me I was going to be in America at least until I graduated from college. If they had, I would have refused to go.

I woke up the day after I arrived and realized how far I was from my mom. Suddenly I felt incomplete, like half of me had died. I started crying. I knew there was no way my father was going to send me back after spending all his money to get me here. But I went to the grocery store anyway, bought a phone card, called my mom, and told her I wanted to return to Kenya.

My mom told me that being in America was better because here I had free education and opportunities most people would die for. My mother's words calmed me down and made me feel a whole lot better. My mom always knew how to convince me—she talked so softly and always made sense to me.

But the calm didn't last. As soon as I hung up the phone I bounced back to being depressed. I started disrespecting my dad, my aunt, and my older cousins. I got into a big fight with my older brother over a cereal he ate. I cursed out my aunt's friends, who said I was a bad girl and that they were happy their kids didn't act like me.

I was mad that I'd left a person I loved and cared about so much, to come to a country I didn't like. I didn't know how to control my anger, so I just let it out on other people. I felt that the only reason I'd done well in school and been a good girl in Kenya was so my mother would tell me she was proud of me. Now that she wasn't with me I felt like there was no one to be proud of me, even if I did good things.

All my brothers were having fun and making new friends. I didn't have any friends at all, and my dad and I were almost like strangers. I slept half of the day and when I finally decided to go out, I felt so out of place that I started to regret it. I always felt lonely—in school, at church, outside. Even when I was home by myself, I felt like I didn't belong.

The kids in school made things worse by making fun of me

because I spoke proper English. I needed someone to tell all this to but I didn't trust anyone, so I kept everything to myself.

The only time I was my old self was when I called my mother. I felt like a little kid every time I spoke to her. She was the only one who could advise me, and make me break down and cry like a baby.

But our relationship gradually changed over the next couple of years. I was a teenager and had so many things bottled up that I needed to get out. But my mom was so far away from me that she was helpless to solve my problems, so I stopped crying on the phone. I didn't want to make her cry every day, thinking about me and my little problems. I felt like I had to grow up and learn to deal with things myself.

I started lying and told her that everything was fine, even though it wasn't. Sometimes my mother sounded like she knew I was hiding something from her. But she would just ask if I was OK and leave it at that, because she knew I only open up when I feel like it. I called her once a week and then it turned into once every two weeks. Even then, I missed being with my mom so much that I would cry when I was alone at night.

One thing I've learned from being in America is that know-

We were broke back in Kenya and sometimes I had only one meal a day, but I had my mom.

ing someone loves you is truly priceless. We were broke back in Kenya and sometimes I had only one meal a day, but I had my mom. Even though I sometimes blamed her for not standing up for herself, now I realize that being near her and loved by her made me want to be a better person.

Here we have money and my father buys me almost anything I want. My dad always says he bought us so many things to make us happy, and it's true: my house is probably the nicest I've seen in America. But there's such a lack of communication that I feel like the loneliest person on earth.

I feel like I need someone to love me. Maybe there are people here who do but I just don't see it, because none of them have had to give up their pride or go hungry so I could eat. Nobody can make me feel loved the way my mom did.

I don't know who I am or who I want to be. I feel torn between wanting to be just as loving and caring as my mom, and not wanting to be hurt like my mom was. I feel guilty for all the things she went through. I know I was young and there was nothing I could do about it, but if I could go back in time, I wouldn't get mad at my mom for every little thing. I'd tell her I truly love her and how lucky I am to have her as a mother.

The writer was 16 when she wrote this story.

At Home Away From Home

By Odé Manderson

A bored mother dwells within my apartment. In between going to school and cooking, she does nothing but bug me. She gets on my case about everything, from college applications to eating knishes.

Mom is heavy-set with a small nose and gray streaks at her temples, giving her an elderly, queen-like appearance. Standing at five-nothing, she may seem like a pushover—until she opens her mouth. As I'm relaxing on my bed, she fixes her hard eyes on me, and bellows:

"Did you send your college application, boy?!"

This question annoys me to no end. My sister, who currently attends college, is the one who knows about my applications. She pushes me to make sure that they are complete. My mom has no idea of what is going on, unless my sister leaves messages for her to give to me, and then she gets on my case.

"Leave me alone," I mutter back.

"Don't talk to your mother like that."

"Leave me alone!"

"Don't talk to—"

She constantly barges into my room, damn near breaking down the door with an attitude over Jehovah knows what, interrupting my peace and privacy to say something irrelevant.

Whatever I don't hide is subject to inspection by her. One time she went looking for something of hers in my room (to this day, she never told me what it was) and ended up "stumbling across" letters written to me by anonymous females.

She gave me the "what the hell are you doing" look before asking a zillion questions like, "Are you buying them things?" or "Why are you even bothering with them?" She feels girls are the root of all evil.

"Don't waste your time, they only want your money. They're nothing but trouble, all of 'em," she says.

"No, they're not."

"YES, THEY ARE!!"

I feel that my mother doesn't respect me. This is a bad feeling to have, knowing what the problem is but being unable to do anything about it. She's my mother, so I can't slam her on the floor like I would any fool who goes to extremes to make my life uncomfortable. When I ask her why she's so disagreeable, she says, "It's just the way I am."

Common sense dictates that if you can leave an undesirable situation, do so. Daily, I travel (or at least contemplate traveling) to my salvation—the house of my good friend David. His crib is probably the only place where I can be myself.

I go there every chance I get because I'm getting too big for my house. At 17, I want to do what I want and make my own choices. My mom feels differently.

She probably forgot what it was like making the transition from being dependent to being independent. When both of us are in the house, the word "peace" is forgotten and is replaced with "turf war."

My mom's ally in the battle is my annoying 13-year-old brother. He sides with the Evil One in getting on my nerves. He sticks his head into my room just long enough to declare me a "skank." I'd like to pummel him out of existence but, unfortunately, the abilities of youth include super speed. Dancing just out of my reach, he spouts variances of his first insult.

At 17, I want to do what I want and make my own choices. My mom feels differently.

"Skank-a-dank, rank, fank, skank!"

I'd rather not deal. So I call up David. As soon as he gives the green light, I stuff a CD into my coat and I'm gone.

"When are you coming back?" is my mother's question.

The slamming of the door is my reply.

"You should disown him," is my brother's snide remark.

"I should," is her response.

It takes 40 minutes to get to David's. I finally reach his block and ring the bell.

"Who is it?" he asks in a thunderclap voice.

"Me," I say through the door. He clambers down the steps. Several locks are sprung, and we're finally standing face to face.

"There's something great on HBO right now," he says over his shoulder as he hops up the stairs. That's our greeting. He's been my friend for more than nine years.

While David and I head toward his room, I hear his mother's voice coming from the living room.

"What's up, Odé?"

"Chillin'," I call out from the hallway. I go over to the couch, where she is casually sprawled in sweatpants and an oversized T-shirt. Looking up at me, she smiles. Her eyes are wide-set, with a scar just above her right one.

"What you been up to?" she asks.

"Trying to get outta school."

"Send out your college application?"

Being asked this question in a tone lower than 250 decibels automatically puts me in a pleasant mood.

"Nah. Not yet."

"Better hurry up, time's runnin' out," she chides smoothly.

Will do, I think to myself as I head toward David's room.

David has been the anchor in my life for a long time. He understands what type of person I was and have become, which makes me more inclined to pick my brain with him than with my mom. Getting my drift is not an all-day affair. I simply tell him what's going on, and he usually agrees with me. When he has a conflicting opinion, it turns into a lengthy conversation that leaves us feeling thoughtful.

It's hard to develop and keep a lasting friendship, but David and I have continually managed to be there for one another during rough times.

When he's slacking in any department, I'm at his house or on the phone coaching him. When the tables are turned, he does the same for me. When I told him about a lifeguard test I had to take last year, he eased my anxiety quickly.

"Well, you're a good swimmer, so don't worry about it," he said. "You'll pass."

And he was right.

One time he had a serious, heated argument with his dad, and I was the first person he called. Of course I readily sympathized, knowing how fathers can be.

But we do have dissimilar ways. I am humorous nearly all the time, even when situations don't call for it, like snapping on someone who wears an orthopedic shoe.

I can also be selfish when it comes to matters of the heart. I feel relationships don't last forever, so wearing my heart on my sleeve when dealing with females is something I don't rush into. In the beginning of a relationship, the most girls get from me is, "You aiight."

David is the exact opposite of this. Within the first few days of knowing a girl, he'll assume he's in love. He'll do anything for her.

"Toughen up, dog," I warn him. "Not all chicks appreciate cats like you. It doesn't make sense to get hurt unnecessarily." He tends not to listen.

David isn't the only person that I look forward to seeing at his house. His mom is low-key and cool as hell. She's never pushy about anything she asks. If I don't want to say anything, she'll understand and go about her business instead of automatically assuming I "had a fight with a girl."

But David says she can be as tiresome as my own mom.

"Daaavid!" his mother calls from the living room.

"What!!" David roars back.

"Do you have clean drawers on?"

My friend David's crib is probably the only place where I can be myself.

But I think David's mom is not nearly as annoying as mine if that's the only thing he has to worry about. I, on the other hand, have to deal with the accusations, the intrusions, the bad attitude, and the lack of respect, trust, and compromise.

Thankfully, my constant battle with my mom will be over in a few months. I'll be 18 and hopefully shipping off to college. But nothing is definite. If I'm not accepted to any of my top picks, I'll attend college at home.

If this happens, David and I plan to be roommates. I can see it now: Waking up to a breakfast of absolutely nothing, scrambling to get our rent money together for the landlord, rushing off to work…then coming home to peace and quiet.

It's a Family Affair

We'll order East Asian and Italian food (Chinese take-out for me and pizza for him). I'll turn the TV on, and we'll kick back and enjoy independent adulthood. Of course, there will be no visitation rights accorded to our moms. And no calling.

But for now, I'm content with making that 40-minute trip to serenity.

Odé was 17 when he wrote this story.
He attended college and majored in writing.

Prisoner In My Own House

By Anonymous

Thirteen was hard. I was insecure about my looks, my mind, and unsure how to act. I was just starting to learn about boys, and finding new and exciting ways to piss my parents off.

Mom and Dad were nice people, but when it came to boys they didn't want to hear about it. They said I had to wait till I was at least 16. Until then, I had to limit myself to school dances.

Their rules couldn't have come at a worse time. The prettiest girl in school had just gotten dissed by the man of my dreams, Raul. He was 17 and, lucky for me, my best friend's neighbor.

At first it seemed impossible to get him to notice me. Those oh-so-pesky zits and the fact that I wasn't allowed to wear make-up really got in the way. But it turned out that Raul saw people for who they really were and not what they looked like.

I started sending him letters and calling him constantly, "just to see how you're doing." He finally got the message and I had my first boyfriend.

It was hard. I wasn't allowed to receive phone calls from males and we couldn't go out in public for fear my parents would see us. Instead we'd hang out at his house or my friend's house once or twice a week. It got extremely frustrating.

After a couple of months, he realized that it was going to be a pain in the butt to go on with the relationship. He called my friend and told her to tell me that it was over. I cried and cried and blamed it on my parents' dumb rules.

About two weeks after we'd broken up, my parents discovered a letter I had written hidden in a box in my closet. It was to my best friend, telling her that it was over between Raul and me, and that J.P., a really cute basketball player, had his eye on me and vice versa.

When I got home that night they were watching TV, acting like nothing was wrong. Then they confronted me with the letter. I was busted. I asked how they found it and my mother said, "I was looking for a pen." (They are even sneakier than I am.)

My father started yelling that I was much too young to go out with anyone. My mom gave me the I-knew-we-shouldn't-have-trusted-you attitude and lectured me on teen pregnancy rates.

They restricted everything I did, from how many phone calls I could get a day to what I wore. (They hated those tight miniskirts.) That didn't stop me though. I changed into my friends' clothes whenever I had the chance and started to cut out of school so I could talk to guys (since I couldn't talk on the phone).

I limited my relationships with guys to hanging out at school, but my parents found out anyway. One night I was talking to my friend Barbara, plotting to stay on the phone so that this guy I liked could call (thank God for call-waiting).

Then her mother needed the phone and we had to hang up. "I'll call you back in 10 minutes," she said. When the phone rang I ran to get it but I missed. My daddy-o picked it up and he didn't quite approve of the masculine voice on the other end. "Who are you?" he barked. "What do you want?"

"Who the hell is Frank?" he shouted.

"A friend from school, Dad," I said.

He hung up on him and told me not to give out my number. Then he launched into that sermon on how I was too young to be involved with guys.

"It's not like you can get pregnant over the phone or anything," I explained. "I just wanted to talk to him."

I spent the next two months cleaning the house and listening to my mother yell whenever I missed a spot. The next time I got to go out I did the ultimate. I ran away. I hadn't planned to—it just happened.

I had gone to the movies with this guy. Being a gentleman, he offered to walk me as close to home as possible and of course I agreed. We were standing on the corner saying goodbye when these car lights shone in my face. I carefully approached the car and my dad told me to go straight home. From the look in his eyes, I thought he was going to kill me.

I panicked and ran after my date. He told me that if I had nowhere to go, I could go to

We couldn't go out in public for fear my parents would see us.

his house. We stayed up all night talking. I couldn't really enjoy myself, though. It was my mother's birthday, and all I could think about was the pain I was putting her through and the way my parents were going to react once I got back.

I went home the next day and they were changing the locks to my room. (They said they were afraid I would have visitors late at night.) My mom was crying hysterically and my dad didn't say one word to me for over a month. He'd send messages through my sister when he wanted me to do the dishes or go to the store.

My parents became true tyrants. They kept me off the phone more, let me go out less (actually, not at all except for school), and had many parent teacher conferences, just to be sure I wasn't cutting.

When I turned 15, they started to let go a little. I could go out with my friends—but only if they had met them and approved. The boy rule still applied until I was 16. I snuck around and got caught a couple more times. But the punishments didn't last forever.

> **I went home the next day and my parents were changing the locks to my room.**

My mom still doesn't trust me. I know it's because she's afraid I'll be a statistic—you know, another teen mother. But I think I've got a pretty good head on my shoulders. My dad sees that and trusts me a little more.

I realize I'm probably wrong for disobeying them. But then, it isn't right for someone to make you feel like a prisoner in your own home.

The writer was in high school when she wrote this story.

She'll Always Be My Mother

By Wunika Hicks

When I look back on my past, I wish I never remembered some of the things that happened to me. My mother was abused as a child, so in return she abused me.

I tried to be the best daughter for her. It just seemed as if she expected so much. I was only 7 years old when I had to stay home from school to take care of my brother. When my brother was born, it seemed like that was when all my problems began.

One day my mother came home after a hard day of work. (Ha! Honestly, I don't know where she was.) She yelled at me as I was feeding my brother David: "Wunika, who told you to give David that bottle?"

I didn't say anything, I just sat in the chair feeding my brother. I wished I could have disappeared. My mother yelled once again: "You're so damn stupid! Put David in the crib!"

It's a Family Affair

I rushed to put my brother in the crib. I never envied my brother so much as at that moment. I wished I could have been in his place. My mother loved him so much. She once told me, "I wish I never gave birth to you." Those words stick with me today.

As I walked back into the kitchen, my mother took the boiling pot of water off the stove (filled with bottles, tops, and nipples I was sterilizing) and threw it in my face. I never yelled so much.

My mother just stood there. She didn't care. All she said was, "Shut the hell up." The skin on my face fell off. I yelled to the top of my lungs. My mother couldn't stand the noise, so she asked me: "Do you want me to give you something to cry for?"

I eventually stopped crying. My mother cleaned my face and boy did I yell! She changed her attitude once she saw the damage she did. She apologized to me.

I never felt so much hate for her. I wanted her to hurt as I did.

When we went over to my relatives' house, all they could say when they saw my face was, "That's a damn shame." I suppose they felt sorry for me. They even bothered to ask my mother why she did that to me, but all my mother said was, "None of your damn business."

I felt so bad for my mother. I thought everything that went wrong was my fault. It seemed as if I couldn't do anything right. I couldn't do anything right at home and I messed up in school.

I felt as if no one cared for me. The teachers always wrote "IGNORE" on the chalkboard because I was the class clown. I had no friends in school because I beat them up all the time. I hated everyone and I fought everything that moved.

One day in school I pulled a chair from under my classmate. The teacher came running. My classmate was crying because when she fell she hit her head on the chair. My teacher looked at me in disgust as she grabbed my arm and put me in my chair.

I went home with yet another letter in my notebook. I didn't have time to tear this one up. To tell you the truth, I forgot about it.

That night my mother opened my notebook to help me with my homework. As she turned the pages she found the letter. SMACK!—right across my face. I fell on the floor. I didn't bother to cry. I did bother to tell my mother that my teacher had grabbed my arm in class.

"WHAT? Who does she think she is? No one puts their damn hands on my child but me! That teacher is really getting out of hand. Wait until I get up to that school, I'm gonna give her a taste of her own damn medicine!"

I was so tickled. I was happy that someone else was going to feel my pain.

I felt so bad for my mother. I thought everything that went wrong was my fault.

The next day my mother took me to school. She busted into my classroom and asked the teacher why she put her hands on me. Boy, was that lady scared!

My mother didn't even give her a chance to speak. BAAM! My mother punched her right in the face. My teacher fell on the floor, the same way I fell so many times before. She was crying on the floor. I began to feel sorry for her. She just lay there, which was a good move because my mother was waiting for her.

Security came and grabbed my mother, and boy was she putting up a fight. The teacher's mouth was bleeding. The children in the classroom watched in amazement. I remember one boy in my class saying, "You and your mother are crazy!"

My mother and I ended up in the principal's office. He told her that the teacher wasn't going to press charges. My mother really didn't care and she did a good job of showing it.

She ended up cursing out the principal. She even threatened to blow up the school and his house, too. I think he believed her from the way he ran to get security. As security escorted my mother and me out of the building, he told my mother not to bring me back. I'm sure you can imagine her response.

Our walk back home was a quiet one. As I stepped inside my room I heard my mother say: "Take off your clothes!" I couldn't believe her. Like any other child, I hesitated. I took my time because I didn't want the beating I was about to receive. My mother became impatient, so she grabbed me.

The only things I had on were my Garfield panties and my tights. There was nowhere to hide. I could hear the belt in my mother's hand say to me: "You again?"

I tried to run but my mother grabbed me by the ankles and beat me as she held me upside down in the air.

That night my mother wouldn't let me sleep with her. I had to sleep on the dining room chairs. We had mice, so I refused to sleep on the floor.

I woke up to David's yells. My mother was gone once again and who knew when she'd return. I picked up my brother from the crib and opened the refrigerator. I took out his bottle and heated it up on the stove. He was still crying, and I felt like killing him.

I wanted to go outside with the kids from my neighborhood, the Fort Greene projects. I got along with the children from around my way. The ones I hung out with all liked to fight.

I searched in the cabinets for David's cereal, to put in his bottle. As I fed him, I couldn't help but wonder if Ma would someday beat him as she beat me. I doubted it. She gave him everything when she was around. He had more than I ever had, from attention right down to the clothes on his back! All I had to my name were one pair of pants and two shirts.

My family knew we were being abused, but they acted like they didn't see it. It was as if we didn't exist, as if we were nobodies. I wanted to hear someone say they loved me. I wanted my mother to say it to me and mean it, the same way she said it to my brother. But how could she claim to love me when she abused me every chance she got?

David sucked the bottle dry. I put him on my shoulder to burp him. Even though I was only 7, I had already promised myself that I'd never have children. I had to admit, though, that

I'd make a damn good mother.

Yuk! David threw up on my shoulder. I hated when he did that. I reached in the closet to get his tub. As I ran his water, David started making noises. I couldn't help but love him. He seemed to be the only one who was thankful for my services.

He loved me. He had to—I took care of him and he depended on me. I had to feed him, change his Pampers, and answer to all his needs. Even though I hated staying home, it was worth watching him.

David loved the water. He never cried when I washed him, but he'd yell when I'd take him out. As I dressed him and combed his hair, I wondered if our mother would be coming home that night. I put David in his crib as I went to run my bath. He yelled at the top of his lungs. I promised him I'd be back soon. I rushed so he wouldn't cry for long.

As I washed up, it brought back so many memories. I remembered my mother leaving me at her girlfriend's house. David wasn't born yet, so I must have been 6 years old. I had to sleep in the same room as the lady's son, who was around 16.

That night he made me sleep in the bed with him. He made me touch his private parts. After that I couldn't remember anything, but I do remember crying to his mother and all she did was smack him.

I was happy that someone else was going to feel my pain.

My mother came to take me home. She told me to take off my clothes so she could wash me up. As she tried to wash my private parts, I'd yell. My mother asked me, "What's wrong?"

I was scared to tell her. I didn't want her to get angry. She asked her girlfriend, "What the heck you do to my daughter?" The lady acted like she didn't know. My mother picked up a chair and threw it at her. The lady started screaming. My mother went to get a knife and the lady finally told her.

That was the first time I saw my mother cry for me. She asked the lady where her son was, but he had left earlier that morning.

My mother then beat the lady the same way she beat everyone else.

David was still crying. I jumped out of the tub and flew to put on my clothes. As I ran to pick him up, I looked at him. He was so handsome—he looked just like my mother.

I felt sorry that he wouldn't grow up with a father. His father left my mother when he found out she was pregnant. He said he was married and couldn't take the chance of his wife finding out. It was as if my mother had bad luck when it came to men. My own father died when I was 2 years old. My mother was never the same after he died. That's what my family said, anyway.

David looked at me as if he knew what I was thinking, because he cried even more. This time I cried, too. Why us? Look at all of those other children—they had a mother and a father. We had nothing. I loved my mother to death but damn, give me a break! I wanted to live my life. Little did I know I'd be sorry when I got one.

> **Look at all of those other children—they had a mother and a father. We had nothing.**

My mother didn't come back home that night or the next. I cried so hard. I prayed nothing had happened to her. I didn't have any food, so I ate some of David's baby food (which wasn't that bad, by the way).

When my mother did return, she came with enough food to last the whole year. She acted as if she'd been gone for an hour. I wanted to question her, but I had to stay in my place.

"Where's David?"

I quickly said, "In the crib." I noticed her looking around the apartment. She asked me, "Did you let anyone in the house while I was gone?" Of course I said no.

My mother fixed my favorite dish, lamb in tomato sauce with rice. I wondered if she was okay. All I cared about was that she was home with me.

As I slept beside her that night, I felt so much safer. I just hoped it would stay that way, that I would always feel safe with her and not be scared. But something deep inside told me that the way we were living couldn't go on forever.

That hurt me. I didn't want my mother to go, just her attitude. I knew if she went away, I'd have nothing. She was a part of me and vice versa, regardless of all the bad things. She will *always* be my mother, I said to myself, just before I fell asleep.

Wunika was 17 when she wrote this story.
She now lives in California with her two children.

Mom, Dad, I Have Something to Tell You

By Jose M. Jimenez

When I realized that I was gay, I knew that I couldn't tell everyone my self-discovery. If I did, I might face serious consequences, like getting homophobic comments hurled at me and getting into fistfights. But I didn't want to keep my revelation all to myself, either. I wanted to share my enlightenment with some of my friends and teachers. And I wanted to eventually tell my parents. I didn't want there to be any big secrets between us.

Yet I didn't feel like I could tell them right away. Though I'd never heard them make homophobic comments, I didn't know how they'd handle my sexuality. I didn't expect anything too bad from my mother, since she's a lot more modern than my father. He's tough and can be really old-fashioned about how things should be done in the house, how children should behave, and how to discipline them. My father is quicker to argue and fight than talk things out with his kids. I thought he'd get angry with me for being gay. I didn't think he'd approve of guys liking other guys.

So instead of telling my parents, I selectively told people I felt I could trust and who would accept me. Telling them was like setting up a safety net for when I chose to tell my parents—I'd be able to turn to them for support if my parents rejected me.

I decided to tell my friends Oscarina, Vanessa, and Belinda first. I knew that they'd be OK with it. Vanessa had helped me realize that I was gay, and Oscarina had told me before that she didn't have a problem with gay people. I knew Belinda would be surprised by the news, which she was, but she dealt with it well.

My English teacher, Ms. Somerville, was the first adult I decided to tell. We'd talked before about what was going on in my life. She was also in charge of the poetry club, where I got to see her more as a friend than a teacher. A few days after figuring out that I was gay, I waited to talk to her after class.

"I'm gay," I blurted out, looking away for a fraction of a second.

I thought that I would be stuck forever in that moment, stuck with that feeling of dread.

"That's great," she said, smiling and giving me a hug. She said it was perfectly normal. She immediately made me feel more confident about who I am.

It felt great to be supported, but I still didn't feel up to telling my parents. After some careful thought I decided to tell my sister Katherine, who's a year older than me. We'd grown close since we were kids, and I occasionally confided in her about my life. My sister has adopted a lot of my parents' viewpoints, so I figured telling her would be a good way to measure how they might react.

"I'm gay," I said one morning in our bathroom as Katherine

used the mouthwash. I got extremely anxious as I waited for a response.

"Hmmm."

Silence.

"I'm not surprised," she finally said after a few seconds. She said she thought I might be and that it was fine. I told her my concerns about our father and she agreed that I should hold off on telling him.

It was a relief to have told someone in my family. There was one less person I had to keep a big secret from. Maybe I'd even be able to talk to her about guys.

I was slowly gaining more confidence about telling my parents. But I was still very worried about how my father would react. So I decided to tell my Aunt Maritza. She's open-minded, and I trusted her to tell my parents for me in a sympathetic way.

When I told her she smiled. She said that she already knew and would handle telling my parents. But this didn't fully solve my problems. While my aunt did indeed tell my parents, I knew that they wouldn't talk about my sexuality with me unless I brought it up first.

I wanted everything to be openly discussed between us, so there wouldn't be any tension. I wanted to be honest about the things I was doing, like working with a gay-related organization.

I chose to speak to my mother first. One day we sat on her bed to talk. I was beating around the subject of my sexuality throughout the entire conversation.

"If you're going to say it, then just say it," she suddenly said. So I told her and she said she wasn't too surprised. I felt relaxed now that I'd told one of my parents. But then she said she wanted me to tell my father.

"You've got to be kidding," I said.

"It won't be as bad as you think," she replied.

I wanted to avoid a hostile confrontation, but my mother insisted.

I held back. But a few days later, while I was getting ready for summer school, I walked into my parents' room to get some lotion. My mother was sitting on their bed. My father was ironing a shirt.

"Tell him," my mother said. I looked at her, surprised and annoyed that she chose this moment to have me do it. I had to leave for school in a few minutes.

"Tell him," she repeated.

I turned to my father, wishing that I could hide. He looked at me expectantly. It didn't seem to matter that he already knew.

"I have to tell you something," I said.

"What? You have a girlfriend?" he said jokingly.

I knew that they wouldn't talk about my sexuality with me unless I brought it up first.

"No, I don't," I answered, only half looking at him. "And you know that I'm not going to have one."

His face grew very serious. I was tense. Time stopped. I thought that I would be stuck forever in that moment, stuck with that feeling of dread. I watched his face closely, waiting for an explosion. Was this the calm before the storm?

But he didn't freak out. We talked for the next five minutes. He was calm and didn't say anything about it being bad to be gay. He just told me that there would be some people who wouldn't accept me, and that I also had to be careful about sexually transmitted diseases like HIV/AIDS.

I nodded that I already knew all this because I wanted the conversation to end as quickly as possible. Now that I'd spoken to him about it, I didn't want to talk about it anymore. All my feelings about being open had flown away. It felt too weird talking to him about my sexuality.

My mother dismissed me, saying that I needed to leave or I'd be late for school. I left happy, knowing that everything had been cleared. I think that my father was so calm because he'd talked to my aunt. He had time to digest the news.

It's a Family Affair

But despite what I'd hoped for, things are far from open in my house. I only talk to my sister Katherine about being gay. It feels too odd to talk about guys with my parents, particularly since my father can be so overprotective. I went to a park the other day just to chill. Because he'd heard that gay men have sex there, he freaked out and started lecturing me. At times like these, I try to tune him out. While he may be trying to protect me, it also shows how he has a lot to learn about me—I don't do sex in parks.

Coming out to my parents was one of the most difficult experiences in my life, but that was partially because I'd expected the worst. I'm pleased with how I went about telling them and thankful I had the support of other people. Still, I'm glad that it's over, and hope I never have to go through something like that again.

---

*Jose was 17 when wrote this story.
He later attended SUNY-Purchase.*

Not Quite a Family

By Anonymous

Here's the story of a lovely lady who was raising one very lovely girl (myself, of course). Then one day the lady met this fellow (with two sons), and they knew that it was much more than a hunch that this group should form a family. That's the way we all became the Rivera bunch.

Unfortunately, the Rivera bunch wasn't a re-make of the classic Brady Bunch story (which consists of two families joining together and living happily-ever-after). If it was, then I would have no story to tell. The Rivera bunch's story has a plot of its own, which I like to call "Life with the Stepfather from Hell."

My mother met Hector (the man who would become my stepfather) when I was 8 years old. At that point, my parents had already been separated for a year. My first impression of Hector was: "He seems like a nice guy, he even treats me nice." He was always complimenting me on how cute I was and how I was such a nice little girl. A couple of times he took me and his sons to a carnival and we went on every ride. We had fun.

After they had known each other for a few months, my mother and I moved into Hector's house. At first everything was pretty cool. I was an only child and now I had Hector's two sons (Frankie, who was 10, and Willie, who was 7) to play with. My first thoughts were: "Wow! I can live with this. Now I'll never feel lonely." I was very happy about the whole thing. I even started calling Hector "Daddy" (something my real dad was not too crazy about).

After a year of living together, Hector and my mother decided it was time to get married. That's when things started to change. After the wedding, Hector stopped being so nice to me.

First, he began comparing me to his sons. I remember one day my new stepbrothers and I were drawing and each of us did something different. Without even looking at my picture, Hector began bragging about his sons' drawings. My mother said, "Yeah, they look good, and look at Angie's. Wow, I'm impressed by all of you."

My stepfather just glanced at mine and continued to brag about his children's artwork. This hurt my feelings because as far as he was concerned, what I created did not matter.

From that day on, I felt the need to be noticed not only by my mom but by Hector too. But the only thing Hector seemed to notice was how his sons were better than me. For example, he would say, "Well, at least my children cleaned their room today."

But when I washed my dishes and Frankie and Willie didn't wash theirs, did I get any credit? No, Hector would just yell at them, "Hurry up, clean it. You guys were never like this, where did you pick up these bad habits?" From me, of course. (The fact that I had washed my dishes didn't seem to matter.)

Most of the time when Frankie and Willie did something wrong, Hector would blame me also. He always found a way to let me know that his children were perfect before they met me (yeah, right).

The only way I could ever prove to Hector that I was worth noticing was with my grades, because I used to always get straight A's in school. But he would only compliment me in front of my mother. I guess I wanted him to really feel proud of me, not just pretend he was when my mother was around. I knew he didn't really mean what he said in front of her, because when she wasn't home he would make fun of me and make me feel stupid.

I wanted him to really feel proud of me, not just pretend he was when my mother was around.

In addition to the way he was always comparing me to his sons, Hector and I had another problem. He wanted my mother all to himself. He just couldn't understand that the love for a daughter was different from the love for a man. He was jealous of me and was always trying to turn my mother against me. Just about every day he would go to her with a different complaint about me.

"Angie didn't clean her room today."

"You know, today Angie was using the phone for more than five minutes."

"She was in the shower for 20 minutes."

"She watched TV all day today."

I would always try to do things right, so he wouldn't have anything to complain about, but he would always find something wrong with me no matter what.

For example, one time after I had done everything I had to do around the house and in my room, I felt like watching TV. When he saw the television on, Hector asked me, "Who turned on the TV?" I told him I did, and he didn't say anything.

I knew I was going to get in trouble because he had a rule that if my stepbrothers or I wanted to watch the TV in the living room, we had to ask him to turn it on for us. But Frankie and Willie always turned the TV on themselves and he never said anything to them about it.

When my mother got home from work, he told her that I turned on the TV without his permission. My mother confronted me and said, "I told you not to touch that TV because that's not yours. If that television were to break, you would be the first person to get blamed."

I answered, "But Ma, he acts like I don't know how to turn on a TV." She responded, "He just doesn't want you touching it, so don't touch it. This way you don't have to hear his mouth." Then she walked out.

Hector started trying to turn me against my mother. Many times when my mom wasn't home, he would complain to me about her flaws. He would say that she didn't treat him as well as she used to. He complained that when she went out, she wouldn't leave a note to say where she was going. He would also complain about her job. He used to say that she paid more attention to her friends at work than to him.

He expected me to keep my mouth shut and just listen.

At first I ignored him, but after listening to him say these things over and over, I started to believe them. Usually the topic was none of my business, but I would get involved anyway because I wanted my mom to be perfect and I wanted Hector to stop complaining. Then my mother would get mad at me for taking Hector's side.

"How could you believe him?" she'd ask me. "I can't believe you would go against me without listening to my side of the story." I would feel so guilty then, but she would always forgive me. It must have really aggravated Hector that each time he tried to turn my mother and me against each other, what it really did was bring us closer together. She would always tell me, "You're the only thing I have. I will never go against you, especially for a man."

But the biggest problem with our new home was that even though I had all the comforts, I didn't feel comfortable. Hector put up a lot of restrictions and they were usually things that stood in the way of the two families really becoming one. For example, when my mother and Hector made separate trips to buy groceries, Hector would place labels on the food she bought to warn his sons not to touch it. That made my mother angry because she felt that everyone should share the food.

Hector was big on labels. He even labeled the phone! It read, "You can't be on the phone for more than five minutes, whether you made the call or not!" When I didn't clean my room he would post signs on my bedroom door about it. I felt like he was trying to drive me out of the house. But I wasn't going anywhere without my mother.

Things went along like that for about three years. Then, when I was 12, Hector started making a real effort to get along with me again, like he had when he and my mom first got together. I think he realized that our problems were affecting his relationship with my mother. He was afraid of losing her and knew that the only way he could make her happy was to change his attitude toward me.

Hector decided it would be easier to start over if we went away on a vacation. We went to Disney World in Florida and we all had a great time. Hector and I didn't have any problems. When we returned to New York, we were still fine. He didn't start anything and I was a good girl. I didn't even mind having him around because he was acting cool again, like when I first met him.

Unfortunately, it didn't last. Hector started picking on me again. He never abused me physically, but he did it mentally. He made me feel bad about myself. Once I overheard him tell someone that I was going to be pregnant by the age of 16 and that I wasn't going to amount to anything because of the way my mother raised me. I never confronted him about any of this, but I feared that everything he said about me was true. Even though I tried to deny it, my self-esteem was on the floor.

The older I got, the more Hector and I argued. He always got mad because I argued back. He expected me to keep my mouth shut and just listen. It's true that I disrespected him many times by talking back, but it was because he never showed me any respect. Once I asked him why he hated me and he responded, "I don't hate you, I just don't like you."

I said, "Well, I don't like you either," and we just left it at that.

The Rivera Bunch was falling apart. Our lives turned into a roller coaster—there were so many ups and downs that all I did was get dizzy. Hector always said I was the reason why his marriage to my mother was in trouble, but I don't think there would've been a problem if he hadn't focused so much attention on me. Maybe he really did think he could drive me out of the house and have my mother all to himself.

If that was his plan it didn't work, because when he drove me out, he drove my mother out, too. They split up four years ago, when I was 15.

When my mother and I moved into a new apartment, it felt as though I was finally set free. But living with just my mother again also took some getting used to. There was a big and constant silence in that apartment.

For a while I missed my stepbrothers, even the screaming and the arguing that went on when we weren't getting along. I was never lonely with them around, even when we fought. I still see Frankie and Willie every once in a while, but the relationship between us just doesn't seem the same. It feels so distant.

Unfortunately I also still see Hector around from time to time, but I no longer speak to him because I don't want anything to do with him.

After reading this story you might have the feeling that

stepfamily relationships are always doomed to failure, but that isn't so. I've seen and heard of many successful relationships between stepparents and stepchildren. In fact, I've been part of one myself. My father also got remarried, and my stepmother and I get along just fine. Not only because I don't live with her, but also because the way she treats me is totally different from the way Hector did.

Every time I sleep over, my stepmother makes me feel very comfortable, and besides that she spoils me like crazy. As soon as I get to her house she starts cooking for me and giving me snacks. She makes me feel wanted and I know she likes having me around. I think if Hector treated me that way—like his daughter, instead of an outsider—then we wouldn't have had so many problems.

The author was in high school when she wrote this story.

My Father: I Want to Be Everything He's Not

By Troy Shawn Welcome

My father was very popular in Guyana, South America, where my family lived until I was 9 years old. His friends used to tell me how it was difficult to walk down the street with him without being noticed. I could only wonder about that because I never spent time with my father when he was around other people. I saw him only on those rare occasions when he slept at home.

My father was what you'd call a playboy. He had a son with one of his mistresses and also a daughter with a second mistress.

But despite all of his faults, I still admired my father. When his friends heard me speak, laugh, or walk, they'd say "that's Terry's son alright." I was just like my dad, and I felt good about that and proud to be like him. He was everything I wanted to be. He was my role model.

In 1983 we came to America. As months passed by, he and my mother fought constantly. I hated when they fought, because he'd hit her. He started disappearing for days and then weeks at a time. For some time I'd only see him on weekends. One weekend, he took my brother and me to a Yankee game. I don't like baseball; the only thing I liked about the game was sitting next to him.

But the thing I remember the most was the weekend when he taught my brother and me how to ride bicycles at the track and field next to Yankee Stadium. I remember going down the straightaway part of the track with my pops at my side. I felt a bond with him.

> *I'd wake up hoping to see him that day, but most of the time I'd be disappointed.*

Those weekends were great, but they didn't last for long. When I was 11, I started to see him less and less each month. I'd wake up on Saturday mornings hoping to see him that day, but most of the time I'd be disappointed.

After about a year he called and asked Rob and me to spend weekends with him in New Jersey, where he was now living. Even though I was happy to be with him, I didn't show it that much. I was hurt because he had left us for so long. It was hard for me to show him that I missed him.

The weekend stays at his house went so well that he asked us to spend the summer with him. I enjoyed that summer. He'd leave money on my pillow before he left for work in the morning. I looked forward to hearing his van pull up when he came home. I felt mad good because I had a dad again.

It was the little things that counted with me. He could have beat me every day for all I cared, and I still would have appreciated it because it was my father who was doing the beating.

The year that followed was good because I saw him almost every weekend. Then one day my father picked my brother and me up and took us shopping in New Jersey. He bought us suits, shirts, and ties, and we went to his house in Newark, where he was living with a woman named Fay.

The house smelled like a bakery and there were a lot of suits lying on the couch. I had no idea what was going on, so I joined two of Fay's sons who were playing video games with some guys from the neighborhood. Suddenly my pops came into the living room, called me and my brother over into the corner, put his arms around us, and said,

"We're going to a wedding on Saturday."

"Whose wedding?" I asked.

"Me and Fay's," he answered.

I had an idea that he'd say that. I was happy for him. I rejoined Fay's sons at the television, hoping to start a conversation because I really felt like I didn't belong. "Yo, you heard... your moms and my pops are getting married?" I said.

"We knew that for a year already, you just found out now?" Shawn asked.

I was embarrassed because my brother and I were the only people who hadn't known. I thought that everyone was laughing at me.

Finally, I raised the courage to call my father up and confront him.

"Now he has new sons and he doesn't need me anymore," I thought.

On the morning of the wedding, my brother and I had to help decorate the hall where the ceremony and reception were to be held. It was hard work, but hours later the hall was transformed with tablecloths and all kinds of decorations. I didn't mind doing all that work because I was looking forward to being a part of the wedding.

But I didn't have anything to do with the ceremony. After it was over, I was still hoping to sit with my father, but I could have waited years for him to notice me. I was disappointed and upset because I did all that work on the hall and didn't get to do anything in the wedding. I felt as though my pops used me as his maid, as though I wasn't important to him.

After the wedding I spoke to my father only when it was absolutely necessary. As years raced by, the number of times that I saw him decreased.

I was angry at my pops for treating me like a stepchild at the wedding, but I still needed him in my life. It was very hard, and still is, to be a teen and my own father at the same time. I'd question whether I was good enough to be considered a man. I couldn't get through a day without stressing myself out about whether I acted, talked, or looked like a man. All that stress affected my life in more ways than one.

Finally, about a year and a half ago, after years of keeping my feelings inside and many, many sessions with my counselor, I raised the courage to call my father up and confront him.

"What kind of father are you?" I asked him. "You don't call, you don't come to see us. If anyone met me in the last two years, they'd think that I didn't have a father. I don't understand what's going on."

"Ah, um, I have been calling and coming by," he countered calmly. "But you are never there."

The way he spoke to me made me feel like we were two executives at a board meeting. "You haven't been calling or coming 'cause I would've gotten a message," I said. "I think it's because you got your new sons and Karen [my older half-sister] over there, so you don't need us anymore."

I was hoping that he'd say that it wasn't true and that he still loved me, but that didn't happen.

"I don't think you should be taking this tone with me," he said. He was starting to get upset. "You call me up and tell me this bull crap about—"

"Bull crap?" I interrupted. "This ain't bull crap. It's the way I feel. I'm telling you the way I feel and that's all it is to you—bull crap!"

"OK, it's the way you feel. But I'm still your father and you shouldn't be speaking to me like this," he said.

"As far as I'm concerned, you're not my father. You haven't been and will never be my father," I told him.

"You will always be my son and we will be together in the future," he said in a patronizing voice.

"If you're not here for me now, what makes you think that I'm going to need you in the future?" I said. "Listen, I have another call so I gotta go, ah'ight."

Click.

How can I love someone I don't know and who doesn't know me?

The conversation pissed me off. First, he had an annoying tone throughout the conversation. It made me feel like he wasn't taking me seriously. Second, he made me realize that I was right—he didn't want me.

But I felt a little relieved at least to know how he felt. It was the hardest thing that I ever did. I was trembling while I was speaking to him. My emotions were so strong from keeping them in for so many years. It was good for me to get them out because now I don't think about him enough to get me depressed anymore.

Surprisingly, he did call me back a few weeks later. He told me that he wanted to hang out with my brother and me that Friday. I canceled my plans just so I could be with my dad.

At 7 o'clock on Friday night I was waiting for him. Nine o'clock came and I was getting frustrated because I hate waiting for people. I finally decided to call and find out if something happened to him. Fay answered the phone and told me he was sleeping.

She woke him up and he gave me some story about having a long day. Then he asked if he could see me on Sunday and I agreed.

To make a long story short, he never came on Sunday. From that day I realized that I was never going to have him in my life again. I've neither seen nor heard from my sperm donor (that's what I call him sometimes) since that conversation—a year an a half ago.

My mother still tries to convince me that I should love him because he's my father. How can I love someone I don't know and who doesn't know me? Today things are better. I've managed to hide my feelings for my father so deep that I'd have to dig to find them. I still think he doesn't want me, but I don't care anymore. I realize that no matter what he did to me, it's no excuse for me to have a messed-up life. Strangely enough he did teach me something.

He taught me that the best man I could be is his total opposite. I now know that having children left and right doesn't make a man. Staying around to raise them does.

I have vowed to my only father, God, that I wouldn't raise my children the way Mr. Welcome raised (or failed to raise) me. I will make it my business to be a part of my future children's lives until I lie in my deathbed. They say that when you get older, you turn into your parents—I pray to God that doesn't happen to me.

Shawn was 19 when he wrote this story. He went to college and graduate school and became a high school principal.

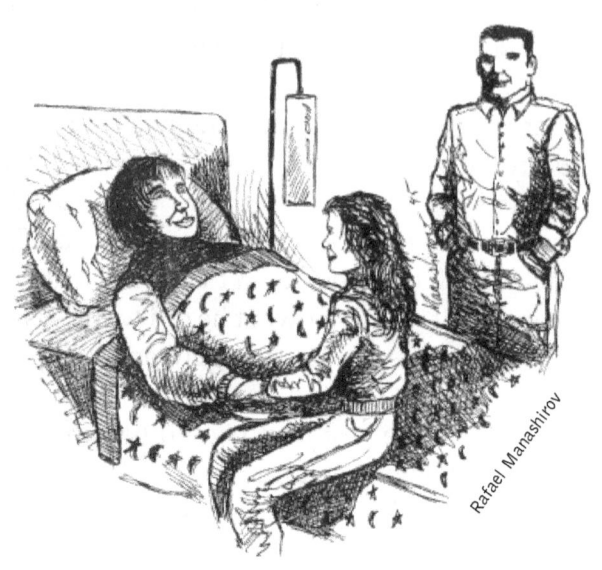

My Mother Almost Didn't Come Home

By Nicolle Lewis

When I was 12 years old, my mother had a stroke. It was the scariest thing that ever happened to me. I didn't know what to do.

It happened one night just as my mother was about to go to work. She was in the kitchen talking to my sister when her face began to look funny. It looked like her mouth had moved to one side of her face, and her eyes looked very tired and droopy.

My sister and I didn't know what was going on. Then my mother told us that she wasn't feeling too well and should call in sick. She didn't go to work that night. Instead, she went straight to the hospital.

I didn't realize that something was seriously wrong until the next day, when my father told us that they were going to keep my mother in the hospital for a while because they had to run a couple of tests.

When I got home from school that day, the rest of the family was getting ready to go to the hospital. I wanted to see my mother so badly, but I was too young. I went along anyway, wondering how they were going to get me up to her room.

When we got to the hospital, my brothers, sister, and father went to the counter to get a pass to go upstairs. They were told that only three people could go at one time and the rest would have to wait for the others to come down. We decided that my sister and two brothers would go and I would sneak in with them.

When we got to her room, my mother was just lying there asleep with tubes in her nose and arms. I couldn't believe what I was seeing. I was scared to go near her because that wasn't the lady I knew. She looked different, lying there so helpless. Her face still looked funny, like her nose and mouth and cheeks weren't where they were supposed to be. My siblings tried to explain to me what had happened to her, why she looked that way.

> *I was scared to go near her because that wasn't the lady I knew.*

The three of them talked to my mother, even though she was asleep. They told her that they loved her, and hoped she would get better and come home real soon. As we were getting ready to go, they asked me if I wanted to say something to her. I couldn't say anything because I still couldn't believe that was my mother lying there. Instead, I went over, kissed her goodbye, and told her that I would be back soon.

We went downstairs and waited for my father to go see her. When he came back, he didn't look good. His face had drooped, as though he'd lost his best friend. He looked very sad and his eyes were watery.

When we got home my father called us into the kitchen for a family meeting. We were all sitting at the kitchen table waiting for the news. Everyone's eyes were pinned on my father except mine, because I didn't want to hear anything bad.

The room was still—just the sound of his voice and us breathing. Then he finally came out and said something like, "You all know that your mother is very sick. The doctors said she might not come home."

I couldn't believe what had just come out of his mouth. I just sat there. A couple of tears fell from my eyes, and then I got up and went upstairs.

When I got up the next morning, I heard my father talking on the phone. He was talking to someone about my mother. I heard him say, "We all went to the hospital and I talked to the doctor about Mary's condition. He said that she isn't doing so well and she might not come home." Then as I closed the door to the bathroom, I heard him say, "OK, Nana, I'll see you later." He had been talking to my grandmother.

I got ready for school with nothing but my mother on my mind. Things weren't the same without her in the house. I missed her waking me up in the morning. I missed hearing the sound of the TV, which she liked to put on before she woke all of us up. I missed smelling the breakfast she usually prepared for us.

Without my mother there, things at my house began to change. Everyone had to clean up, cook, and go food shopping—stuff my mother had always done for us. My sister and sister-in-law did the cooking, and the food did not taste as good as when my mother fixed it.

Days went by and there was still no change in my mother's condition. We went to the hospital every day, and I prayed every night for the Lord to look down and change what was happening. "What would it be like around here if we lost her?" I thought. The house would always be dirty, things would always be out of order, family nights wouldn't be fun anymore.

After my mother had been in the hospital for about six weeks, her doctor called our house. Part of me wanted to eavesdrop, but I was afraid he would say something I didn't want to hear. Like that my mother had passed away.

Instead, he told my father that she was doing much better. They had figured out what caused the stroke. It was related to the fact that my mother had diabetes and had not been taking care of herself. She was not supposed to eat sweets, but she is very hard-headed and ate a lot of cakes, pies, and other things that she was not supposed to have. This made her blood pressure go up, which was very dangerous.

When my father got off the phone with the doctor, he told all of us the good news. She was going to be OK. That day I made all kinds of things to decorate her room—pictures, posters—and everything said, "Get Well Soon."

That night we all went to the hospital. I couldn't wait to see my mother's face. When we got in the room she was sitting up watching television, waiting for us. She still had the tubes in her arm and her face still looked a little funny, but she seemed much better.

My brothers and sister all hovered over the bed kissing and hugging her. I stood in the back, waiting my turn. My mother asked, "Where's Nikki?" They all said, "Right here" and turned around and there I was.

I ran up and gave her everything I'd made. She grinned and told me she loved me and missed me so much. I sat on the bed next to her and hugged her as tight as I could and wouldn't let go. I asked her when she was coming home and she told me, "Soon." I couldn't wait for that day to come.

When I first realized that I might lose her, I felt like I was falling and no one was going to be there to pick me up.

We hugged my mother goodbye so my father could spend some time with her. When he came down his face looked overjoyed, like he had just hit the jackpot. He came over and told us that our mother would be coming home in two days and that a nurse would come to our house twice a week to help take of her. I was so happy all I could do was smile.

It's a Family Affair

The day my mother was coming home, I sat on the porch waiting for her. Finally, a car pulled up in front of the house and a lady dressed all in white stepped and came around to open the passenger door. Then I saw my mother's face. I ran to help her out. I yelled, "Mommy's home" and everyone came to the door.

We walked her into the house and straight upstairs to her bedroom. The nurse helped her get ready for bed and told us that our mother needed a lot of rest and no aggravation. I went downstairs, fixed her some soup and crackers, then took it upstairs and watched her eat it. Then I combed her hair and put on the TV and left her to rest.

It took my mother another seven or eight weeks to recover completely. I was so happy to have her home where she belonged. I prayed every night for God to bless her and keep her with us for many more years. I knew that she could have another stroke if we didn't help her take care of herself.

I had always been close to my mother, but after she got sick we got even closer. When I first realized that I might lose her, I felt like I was falling and no one was going to be there to pick me up. I was young and wouldn't know how to survive without her. Who would I talk to about boys, about getting my period, about what bra size to buy? You can't go to your father and talk to him about those kinds of things.

Six years have passed, but I still think about the time my mother was lying there helpless and struggling to get better. When I think about it, I just sit there and start to tear up. I feel relieved that she is here today, that I still have someone to call "Mommy." I thank God for sparing her life and letting her see me grow up to where I am now.

Nicolle was 18 when she wrote this story.
She earned a bachelor's in journalism and a graduate
degree in media arts at Long Island University.

He's Not My Grandpa!

By Megan Cohen

When I was in elementary school I was afraid of telling my friends my parents' age. My parents, who'd had me when my mom was 40 and my dad was 46, always seemed to be so much older than my classmates' parents that I felt almost ashamed.

When my father took me places, people would ask him if I was his granddaughter. My father didn't care. He'd laugh and say, "No, she's my daughter, can you believe it?" I'd feel humiliated, though, and just look at the ground intently. I didn't want to have a father who looked like a grandfather.

Not only was having older parents embarrassing, it was boring. I saw other parents playing with their kids, and they were more energetic than I had ever seen my parents be. I wanted to have fun, too. But half the time I was too active for my parents.

Once when I was about 6, I was at the beach with my mom,

dad, and 19-year-old sister. I kept begging my parents to play.

"Mommy, Mommy, do you want to go swimming with me?" I asked.

"Maybe later. Ask your father, maybe he'll go," she suggested as she sat back, half-asleep in her chair. She wasn't doing anything, so why couldn't she come and play?

"Daddy, will you go swimming with me?"

"Not right now. Go ask your sister," he said, blowing me off completely so he could read the newspaper.

Annoyed, I gave up and instead built a sandcastle on my own. After a long series of experiences like that, I learned to play by myself more often. I'd read and play games using my imagination. But I'd also watch other families running around and playing together and wish I had a family like that. Two fun parents, with siblings young enough to play with.

Back then I thought that having older parents meant there was no way I could connect to them. They couldn't understand me because they'd forgotten what being a kid was like.

I was in a world of dolls and imagination while they were in another, much older, world that consisted of nothing but talking. I always felt a little guilty if I liked a kid thing, like cartoons. I was afraid my parents would tease me for liking something that was so obviously stupid.

I also thought having older parents made it harder for me to relate to my peers. I grew up in a more old-fashioned and adult culture than other kids my age. I listened to older music—Frank Sinatra and Sammy Davis Jr. from my dad, and a lot of Buddy Holly and '60s hippie music from my mom. And, during our unit on the stock market in 5th grade, I'd occasionally correct my teacher, since news about the stock market was always on in our house.

In some ways my sister, who's 13 years older than me, had a different childhood than I did, though we have the same parents.

She says that my parents haven't changed, but when she was a kid they were still fairly young.

They were never exactly athletic, but I do know that when my sister was younger they'd go bike riding together. The one time I saw my parents ride a bike, I didn't breathe the entire time—I was too afraid they were going to hurt themselves.

Also, they were a little more involved with her life. They went out a lot more, participated in her school activities, and were friends with her friends' parents. And my sister grew up when my parents had more time and money to devote to her.

With me, they had "second kid syndrome." They'd been there and done that (with my sister), and didn't feel the need to be as involved in my life.

My sister didn't have to cope with hospitals at a young age either, like I did. When I was 4 my father had a stroke. It messed with his brain a bit, and when he returned from the hospital weeks later, he acted completely different for a few years.

A few months after my father's stroke, my mother went away on a business trip and my father was left to take care of me. I was getting ready for preschool in the morning, and my dad told me to hurry up. Then, as I was finishing putting on my shoes, he said that he didn't have time to wait for me and left.

They'd forgotten what being a kid was like.

I waited around for a minute for him to come back, as I expected an adult should do. Then, when he didn't, I ran down the hallway looking for him, to see if he'd really had the audacity to leave me. He had.

I started to cry. I couldn't believe my father had deserted me. I couldn't stay home by myself. My mom wouldn't want me alone at home. But what could I do?

Then I saw my grandparents' phone number taped to the fridge, and I called to see if my grandfather would take me to preschool. (Though he was about 80, aside from using a cane he was in pretty good health.) He kept his cool and came right over, and everything turned out fine.

But circumstances like those made me grow up a little faster. I began to see my father less as someone who could take care of me, and I began to take care of myself more, which was annoying because I felt that was his job.

But as I got older, I began to see the advantages of having older parents. In elementary school when other kids' younger parents were divorcing, I found it foreign. I couldn't imagine parents separating.

That was because by the time I was born my parents had been married for 14 years already and were settled in life. They both had steady jobs, my dad as a pharmacist and my mother working for a successful company for about 15 years.

As I got older, I began to see the advantages of having older parents.

Their marriage seemed just as steady. Though they bickered with each other, they always made up quickly and were basically dependent on each other for everything. They had already been through the worst with each other and hadn't split up, so I never worried they would.

I also noticed that some of my peers' young parents seemed like they'd never fully grown up. Some of them acted more like friends to their kids than parents. I remember that when my cousin fought with his young father, his father's way to resolve the argument was by starting a wrestling match.

And my friend and her mother, who's probably about 20 years younger than my mom, have smoked pot together. That seems like an abnormal thing to do, and one bonding experience I know I'll never have with my mom. (For starters, she gets flustered after a glass or two of wine.)

When I was 11 and wanted to go to sleepaway camp, I chose the camp, filled out the forms. and all but handed over the money—most of my peers' parents did this for them. I think

I was mature enough to do it because I'd been depending on myself since I was young.

So, while having older parents used to bother me, and sometimes still does, I've begun to see there were some positives. Also, all the things that made me feel out of place before just make me worldlier now. I'm glad to know both the old and new in music and movies. And my childhood knowledge of the stock market is finally paying off. Now some of my more entrepreneurial friends turn to me for investment advice.

When I was younger, I felt like I was older than my years because of my older parents. Now I'm finally on the same page as my peers.

Megan was 16 when she wrote this story.
She later attended McGill University.

Mom's Rules Make Me Feel Trapped

By Anonymous

I'm 18 years old, and my mother calls me every hour on the hour because she wants to know where I am and what I'm doing. She knows all my friends and has all their numbers. My friends crack jokes about my mom being overprotective. Even her sisters and brothers think she's too strict with me.

One night when I was 15, my cousin and I wanted to see a movie, but my mom said no because it started at 9 p.m., which she thought was too late. She let me go bowling instead. I was spending the night at my aunt's house, and we got back around 11 p.m.

"Your mom was calling here breaking," Aunty said when we walked in the house. "I just got off the phone with her."

I tensed up. Whenever I went to someone else's house, my mom would call and argue about where I was with whoever picked up the phone. "Why was she so upset? She knew where I was at," I said.

"Uh huh, but your mother said you're a liar because you weren't in the house before 10 p.m.," Aunty answered.

"What? How am I a liar? I went bowling. We had to wait a hour for a lane to open up," I protested.

"Your mother thinks you went to the movies after all, and she said to come home tonight," Aunty said. "Girl, I don't know how you do it. If I had a mom like yours, I'd jump out the window. I'd probably strangle her. What's your secret?"

I laughed, but inside I agreed with Aunty. Sometimes I did want to strangle my mom.

My mother believes that a girl isn't grown until she's 21 years old, and the only way to raise a child is to have strict rules and discipline for all 21 of those years. I'm my mom's only child, and I don't see my dad much at all. Mom says that she wants to protect me from "the big bad world." She says she doesn't want things that happen to people on the news to happen to me.

My mother calls me every hour on the hour because she wants to know what I'm doing.

But her rules make me feel suffocated and trapped. At times I feel like telling her off, but when I do, she talks over me or yells at me. I get the urge to scream back, but I don't. Sometimes I even want to push or hit her. I want to tell her, "Leave me alone and let me breathe."

I believe that she loves me because she worries about me so much. But that's all she does. She doesn't want to hear about my life, and we don't say much to each other except, "How are you?" and, "Fine." I wish she'd put more energy into supporting me instead of controlling me.

I understand some of her concerns for my safety, though. We live in a dangerous neighborhood where people often get shot. Every other corner is a hot spot where people are dealing drugs.

But my mom taught me to stay away from dealers and the bad corners. Plus, everyone knows me in my neighborhood and they don't let anything happen to me. I've always done well in school, never gotten involved in drugs or drinking, and haven't gotten pregnant. But even now, Mom doesn't trust me to go on a date.

One time she told me she doesn't want me to make the same mistakes she made in life, but she's never told me what those mistakes were. How am I not going to make the same mistakes she made if I don't know what they are?

Her rules make me feel suffocated and trapped.

Until I was 15, my curfew was 8 p.m. Mom didn't let me go out with my friends or take the subway without an adult. I couldn't pick out my own clothes, and I wasn't allowed to date or even get calls from boys.

She never told me how she would punish me if I broke a rule, but she said that she'd find out if I was disobeying her. I was afraid that she'd beat me if I did something wrong, because she hit me a few times when I was younger.

When I was 15, I was so desperate to escape mom's rules that I decided to run away to my dad's. I packed a suitcase and hid it under my bed, waiting for the right moment. But mom saw it and confronted me after school one day. She asked me what was wrong and why I wanted to leave. She said I didn't love her.

"I love you," I told her. "You just make me mad and you get on my nerves."

"How do I get on your nerves? What do I do?"

"You're always yelling at me. You call me every hour. You barely let me go out with my friends. You are too overprotective."

"I call you because I worry about you and I want to make sure you're OK," mom said. "I don't want anything to happen to you. And I'm not that overprotective. I let you go out."

"No, you don't. I go outside around the block or to my cousins' house. I don't get to go to the movies and stuff like that unless it's with an adult."

I explained that I wanted her to extend my curfew and to stop calling me at other people's houses. I also told her I wanted us to talk more. I think it really scared Mom that I was thinking of leaving. Usually she's the boss and whatever she says goes, but this time she listened.

After our fight, she changed a little. She started to let me go out with my friends without an adult present. She changed my curfew to 9 p.m. on my 16th birthday, and she let me shop for myself. I was relieved that she let me have some freedom, and I felt she cared about my feelings.

But not long after that fight, my mom wouldn't let me apply to a high school in another part of the city because "it's too far. I don't want you to be going to school out there by yourself."

Part of me thought she was afraid of me leaving because I'm her only child and she'd be lonely without me. That's a kind of love, but the kind that feels like jail.

I went to my zoned high school and joined the basketball team freshman year. I loved it, and wanted my mom to come to my games, to be a part of something that I enjoyed doing and that I was good at.

She would say she'd come but never did, even though I sometimes had games on days she didn't have to work. It felt like a knife in my heart when she didn't show up. She loved me so much that she wouldn't let me leave her side, so how could she leave me hanging when I wanted her with me?

With my mother acting like my jailer instead of my mom, I ended up doing exactly what she didn't want me to do: I started dating boys behind her back.

"You better not be having sex. You better not have a boyfriend. You can't date," mom would tell me. "You're not going to be like those young girls out there having babies. You're going to graduate and be something in life."

But her words didn't stop me from going out with Michael, my first real boyfriend. We met when I was a freshman in high school. He showed up at my basketball games and went to church with me even though he didn't have to go. I could talk to him about anything.

But I constantly worried that my mom would find out about us, and if she did, she would forbid me from seeing him. Finally, after two years, the hiding got to me. I broke up with Michael. I haven't had a boyfriend since then, and I don't want one until I get out of the house.

My mom loosens her rules slightly each year. Now that I'm 18, my curfew is 11 p.m. I can take the train and the bus by myself if I have to. But her attitude towards me hasn't changed. She still has to know everywhere I go and who I go with. She calls me on my cell phone all the time to see where I am. She tries to tell me what I can and can't wear, and I'm still not allowed to date.

*I*nstead of worrying about my physical safety all the time, I wish my mom were more emotionally protective of me. I want to be able to ask her for advice. I also want her to open up to me.

Even though my mother drives me crazy, she's the only mom I've got. That's why it hurts me that our relationship is so much about rules, and so little about communication and closeness.

Sometimes I think I should sit down with her and, without seeming disrespectful, explain how I feel.

But I'm scared she'll freak out and start yelling. Every time I want to talk to her, it's like my mind goes blank and the words won't come out.

I plan to go away to college in a year, and I look forward to getting away from mom and her rules. I believe I'll feel free and more at ease. But I still want to be close to my mother. I don't want to feel like we could never break down the walls between us.

The writer was 17 when she wrote this story.
She majored in liberal arts at LaGuardia Community College.

My Parents Gave Me Everything—Except Themselves

By Lily Mai

I used to think my parents didn't love me because they seemed to value money more than they valued me. Maybe I was wrong, but when I was little, all I noticed was that they weren't around.

When I was young, my parents worked up to 14 hours a day, so my grandparents raised me until I was 7. They worked so hard because we were poor. The Chinatown apartment I shared with my parents, brother, and grandparents was extremely small, with just two rooms and a kitchen.

The bathtub was in the kitchen and the bathroom was in the hallway outside the apartment. My grandpa taught me to kill the roaches that were everywhere by pouring hot water on them.

My Parents Gave Me Everything—Except Themselves

The refrigerator was never cold enough, the stove was covered with grease and the kitchen wall was so spattered with cooking oil that my parents had taped calendar paper over it. My grandparents slept in one bedroom, which doubled as the living room, and my parents, brother and I slept in the other.

At the time, it didn't bother me that we had so little, or that my parents were always at work (my father was a chef in a Chinese restaurant and my mother made clothes in a factory). My grandparents gave me everything to keep me satisfied. They took my brother and me to the park, school and McDonald's. They bought us picture books and crayons, washed our hair and even potty-trained us.

But when I was 7, my parents had saved enough money to move. My parents, brother and I left my grandparents' apartment in Chinatown and moved to a big three-bedroom house in Brooklyn. It was nice at first because my parents were able to buy a new stove, TV, and new furniture.

But without my grandparents around, I began to notice the long hours my parents worked to pay rent and to buy the furniture.

It seemed like money was the only form of communication in that house.

They had only one day off a week, and they usually spent it paying bills or shopping for things they needed. They didn't talk to or play with my brother and me.

When my mom was around, her role seemed to be to keep me out of trouble and make sure I did my homework. My relationship with my father was no better. He just gave us money and bought us food. It seemed like money was the only form of communication in that house.

I tried to come up with things to do on my own. I played with my Barbies, watched TV, and built tents in the living room. But I would've given up the big house and TV and gone back to live in Chinatown if I could have had my parents around. I was lonely.

It's a Family Affair

My parents had given me money, clothes, and food. But these were poor substitutes for love and attention.

Last summer, when I was 16, I finally realized just why they were so focused on money. We took a trip to China and went to visit their childhood homes. That's when my feelings about them began to change.

I'd always known my parents had a rough childhood. They'd told me things like, "If there was food on the table, then it was a good day." But I couldn't imagine their childhood until I actually saw where they grew up.

When we got to the farm where my mom grew up, in a small town near the city of Guangzhou in southeastern China, I saw that the ground was nothing but dry soil. It was like a desert with leaves, trees, and roads of endlessness ahead.

There were old gray brick houses and roosters making cock-a-do-da-do noises from wooden cages. The heat was unbearable and made me itch. I kept swatting flies off my skin, and everywhere there was the sound of insects. I wanted to get away fast. I wished I'd never come.

Then I entered my mom's old house. It had two bedrooms, a kitchen in the living room and a second floor dedicated to praying. The beds were made of flat wooden planks. There were no couches, just a row of chairs.

My mom said they'd leave the door open every day because they lived in a deserted area, and dogs and roosters would come in and walk around the living room.

The stove was a box of gray bricks and there were logs under two huge holes where they'd build a fire and put a pot over it to cook. There were no machines to make things like ladders, pots or chairs, so they made them by hand instead.

They had to kill animals and grow vegetables to eat. It was like living in the 17th century. I was amazed. I thought, "This is what poverty looks like."

My mom told me how in the mornings she'd go to school

and learn how to read and write Chinese characters. When she got home, she'd scrub the kitchen walls or help her mother make dinner, peeling off chicken feathers and putting her hand inside the chicken to remove the insides.

Or she'd wash her clothes on the porch, leaning over a bucket of water and a bar of soap on the floor. Afterward she'd make a fire and cook for my grandmother. There was no TV, CD player or computer so her days were spent doing things to get by. That was my mother's childhood.

It was worse than I'd expected. I wanted to look away because I felt guilty about my childhood compared to my mother's. I hoped my mother was too busy catching up with her relatives and friends to see my reaction. We visited my dad's house nearby too, and it was even smaller than my mother's.

I think in trying so hard to save me from the life she had as a child, my mom overlooked something.

I thought about my own home. I had my own room with my own TV, computer, and a comfy bed. I had lots of clothes to wear. I had an education. Suddenly I realized why they'd risked everything and left their relatives behind to come to a new country where they didn't speak the language, and get jobs working 14 hours a day. They did it to give me all the things they never had. Maybe they did love and care about me after all.

There've been times when I've dreamed of one day getting away from my parents and living independently. I've imagined not inviting them to my wedding or sending them money when I grow up, thinking that then they'd realize how much they hurt me. I wanted to use money against them since it seemed to be more important to them than love.

But now I see that the money they worked hard for six days a week wasn't for them, but for me. I'm grateful for the long hours they worked and the money they saved to give me a better life. I hope I can pay them back when I get a job. I hope one day I can buy them something big like a car or a new house.

Still, I think in trying so hard to save me from the life she had as a child, my mom overlooked something. She told me how hard she worked growing up. But she also said how she worked alongside her mother and had long conversations with her.

I think that's how they developed the bond they have now. Today, my mother talks to her mother about almost everything. They joke with each other and talk for hours about work, friends and movies. My father has a good relationship with his parents too. They read the newspaper together and talk about the news.

I hardly talk to my parents at all, and I can't imagine laughing with them the way my mom does with her mom. Sometimes I wish I could trade in some of the things she gave me as a child for a few of the hours of closeness she and her own mother had.

I don't think my mother realizes how important love and affection is to me. I think she and my dad thought that by working and buying me things, they were showing their love for me.

My parents grew up in poverty, and they worked hard so I wouldn't experience the same thing. They did a good job—I grew up in comfort and didn't struggle to survive. I had so many things. The only thing missing was my parents.

Lily was 16 when she wrote this story.
She attended Brooklyn College.

Her Shining Star?

By T. Garrido

My boyfriend Antonio and I sat on the bus, and I held my sweaty hands together, a glaze of thoughts about the school day running through my head. Teachers sure had a way of making 8th grade seem like the most devastatingly important year of your life.

I looked back at Antonio only to catch him staring at my mouth, which struck me as odd. As I was about to look away, he grabbed my chin and planted a soft yet strong kiss on my lips.

I was shocked. It was only my second kiss ever, and I didn't like that he chose that moment on the bus to do it. But we could never kiss anywhere else since I wasn't allowed to date. My mother had strict rules about things like that.

Actually, she had strict rules about everything. I'd never been allowed to see my friends after school or invite them to my house. My mother said it was because our apartment was too small, but I wasn't allowed to go to their houses, either.

I don't know why she was so protective of us, but it seemed like I was the only kid who couldn't hang out with my friends or go to sleepovers. I couldn't even go to the store alone because she worried something might happen to me. My mother made me feel safe, but at the same time I was upset that I couldn't do the things that other kids were doing.

Despite this, my mother and I were extremely close. I was her shining star, who she'd brag about to anyone who would listen, and she was my hero. We spoke about everything I was curious about, like the menstrual cycle and male body parts. She never denied me answers. She always told me the truth so I wouldn't have to find out from a stranger.

But when I started middle school, I began to feel out of place. Girls wore makeup and had cell phones and purses instead of book bags. They also had boyfriends. They laughed at me because my mom brought me to school and picked me up every day. I thought, "I have to do something or they're going to think I'm a mama's girl."

When I met my first boyfriend, Antonio, in 8th grade, I felt like I was finally growing up. My mother liked Antonio and she allowed us to talk on the phone and for him to walk me to the bus after school. But we were never allowed to be alone together, even at school, since my mom worked there. Eventually Antonio wanted to get more physical and I wasn't ready for that, so we broke up. But our fateful kiss on the bus would soon lead to my obsession with public displays of affection.

I was tired of all the rules. I had spoken to my mom time and time again about allowing me to go to the movies alone or to the park, but she always said I was too young. I was angry that she wouldn't meet me halfway like she'd do for some things, like deciding the time I could stay up past my bedtime. For this, she would not budge.

I decided that if she wouldn't allow me to date, I would do it behind her back. I started going out with a lot of boys and kissing them on the bus, which was a convenient place to do it without my mother finding out. At first, I only did it to get boys excited. It was like waving a piece of meat in front of a hungry dog.

But eventually, I began to feel an adrenaline rush when I did it. I was sharing a private moment with everyone else, whether they wanted to see it or not. I felt powerful.

I knew it was wrong but I couldn't stop. I felt like as long as I kept doing this every afternoon, I would never lose my high. What started out as a way to avoid my mom's rules became an obsession. I wasn't just breaking her rules anymore—I was doing something against everyone's rules. I felt free.

For the next year and a half, I went through a stream of nearly 10 boyfriends and made out with each of them on the bus, sometimes even groping each other's private parts.

At home I still did my chores and talked innocently about boys. My mom and aunt, who lived with us, didn't seem to suspect anything. I thought I'd found a way to be accepted at home while escaping my sheltered life. I felt a little guilty for misleading my mom and disrespecting myself by doing a private thing in a public place, but I was more concerned with having fun and doing what I wanted. Never did I think it would affect anyone but me. I was wrong.

I was angry at myself for leaving the diary at home, and for betraying my mother.

One day during sophomore year when I got home from school, I could feel a tension in the apartment as soon as I opened the door. Usually I was greeted with hugs and a "How was your day?" but that day I saw no one. I walked into my room and saw my underwear drawer wide open. I knew what was coming next.

I walked into my mother's room and everything around me went black. I felt frozen in time. My mother was sobbing with her head down and my aunt was staring at the light blue cover of my diary on the bed. She never looked up, just stared at the

It's a Family Affair

words "Drama inside, beware" that I'd written on the cover one day when I was bored. It went downhill from there.

My diary contained detailed descriptions of my many brief relationships and our actions on the bus. I was furious. How could they be mad at me when they had read something they weren't supposed to? My diary was private for a reason.

Then I began crying, imagining the disappointed tears my mother must have shed while she read all that her baby had done. No one said anything. I just walked slowly out of her room and into mine. I took off my clothes, still shocked, and went to bed.

I woke up early the next morning, feeling numb. I walked into the hallway to see the golden light escaping from under the door of my mother's room and I got up the nerve to ask if I could talk to her. I could tell she'd been crying by the tremble in her voice from behind the door. In a hushed tone, she said, "I think everything has been said. There's nothing you could say now to change anything."

I had never heard her this way with me, like she was a robot. When she was upset with me she always talked to me, or if she was really upset, she might yell. Her tone made me feel like I had done something I couldn't fix.

My tears formed a natural disaster on my face as I walked away. I was upset that I had deceived her and I was hurt that she wouldn't talk to me. I was sorry for making her feel this way. I just hoped she knew that. But as time went on, it became clear that she didn't.

For three months my mother and aunt didn't talk to me. Each time I tried to apologize, my mom ignored me. I had to cook meals for myself, and the only one who spoke to me was my sister. It was hell. I lay in bed reading so much that I suffered from back pains. My heartbeat quickened every time I heard my mom's bare feet hard and quick on the wood floor of the hallway. Each time she passed my room I thought this time I would speak to her. But each time, she would walk by swiftly and slam a door. My countless letters asking her to talk to me, placed neatly on her table or in the kitchen, were left unanswered.

There were days when I was angry at myself for leaving the diary at home, angry for doing those things that I knew were unacceptable, and for betraying my mother and losing her friendship.

But I also felt that I wouldn't have done this in the first place if my mother had let me have a little bit of a life outside of school and home. And I was angry that her silent treatment went on for so long. I felt like she didn't care about my feelings, like all she thought was that I had done this to her and that I deserved what I got. I cried so much that my face had an almost permanent puff to it.

Finally, my mother came home one day and found another one of my letters in her room. She barged into my room and answered one of the questions that had been in all of my letters: "What exactly are you upset at?"

"You know why I'm sad? Huh?" she said. "Because I am burying my little girl. I don't have a little girl anymore."

This shocked me. I felt like she wanted me to be the angelic little girl I once was. She wasn't ready for me to grow up and be imperfect. We both began crying and all I wanted to do was give her a hug, but I didn't dare to get up. I couldn't stand being rejected. She asked me, "Why?" and, "How could you do this to me?"

At first I felt like saying, "I didn't do anything to you, I did this to myself. I'm the one dealing with disrespecting myself and hurting my pride and lowering my standards." I was angry at myself for all these things, but I was also angry that my mother thought I was deliberately trying to hurt her.

I told her that I never even thought about hurting her but that I was rebelling against not having a life. "Mom, you don't let me do anything by myself or go anywhere," I said. "I'm an outcast. No one invites me anywhere because they know my mom won't let me go. I'm too old for that."

She said she understood but still expected me to abide by her rules. I was so happy to be talking to her again that I didn't argue, and we left things on a civil note. But there was still a lot of work to do. She still couldn't trust me and I understood why.

About a month later, my guidance counselor gave my mom an application for an after-school/summer program, saying it would be a good thing to put on my resumé. I already had an application, but I had assumed my mom wouldn't let me do it so I never bothered asking. But to my surprise, my mom filled it out right away and allowed me to participate.

She had never let me join anything before, ever. It was especially unexpected since we still weren't on the best of terms. I felt like she was trying hard to meet me halfway. I could tell she wasn't very sure of her decision, but she was trying to let go and trust me. This was new for both of us.

I was rebelling against not having a life.

After that, my mother and I decided to start going on what we called "dates" about once a week over the summer. We'd go to brunch or dinner and talk. We'd always talked, but now we were both making an effort to understand each other.

One night we sat in a diner for more than three hours, talking about what had happened in depth for the first time. She sat across from me, slowly eating her western omelet and sipping her coffee, her eyes sparkling in the dim light. During that conversation she never condemned me. She never stopped me and said, "I don't want to hear any more." She listened and encouraged me to continue talking. She smiled when I told her, "Mom, sometimes I felt like telling you about what I was doing but I just didn't know how."

"Baby, when you have something to tell me, no matter how bad, just say it and I will listen," she said. "I would rather you tell me like that than not tell me at all."

I wondered if it would have been that easy had I gone to her earlier. Maybe not. I think it took something pulling us apart to bring us closer together. I feel like it's the only way she could understand how important it was to me to have some freedom. But I do believe now that as long as I'm the one who tells her, she will always listen and try to understand.

Even though she's still protective when it comes to dating (she has asked me not to date anyone until I've gotten to know them well), she has learned to let go in other areas. I think that's because she sees that this experience has helped me grow up and learn to think before I act, so she doesn't need to be so strict with me.

She used to not let me do anything after school. Now I can spend time with friends as long as it's not late and she knows where I am. Most importantly, she encourages me to follow my dreams and join programs that enrich me, like the after-school program, where I've been studying graphic design and creating pieces of art that I once would have thought impossible. I made so much progress there that I won an award for professionalism last summer.

I remember when I got my acceptance letter for a writing internship last spring, I ran upstairs to show my mom. There were tears in her eyes as she hugged me and told me over and over again how proud of me she was. I thought that internship would be it for me, but she encouraged me to apply to the Reader's Digest Journalism Training Program, too, and I also got accepted to that.

My mother and I have not only built trust, we have built a stronger, healthier relationship. I am proud of her for encouraging me to explore my world and experience new things even though it's hard for her to let go. She has not limited me to anything but the sky. And she says I can have that, too, if I really want it.

The writer was 17 when she wrote this story.

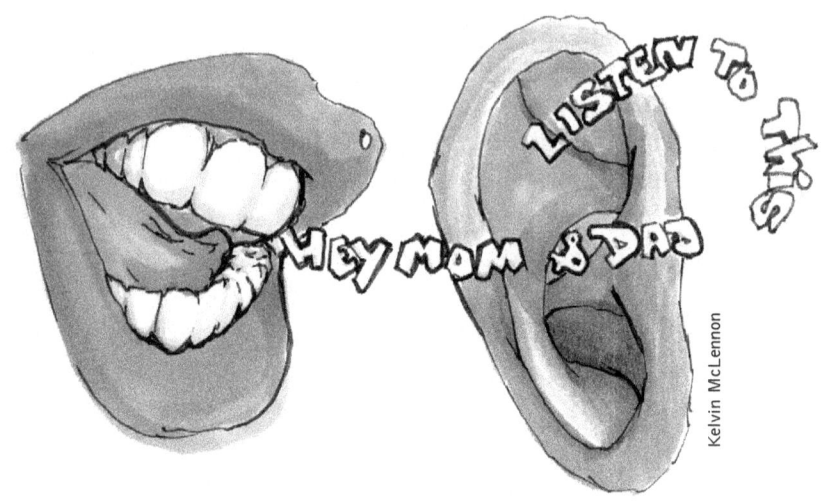
Kelvin McLennon

Communication: How to Get It Started

By Anonymous

For a long time, I have been trying to find a way to be closer to my parents. But I think I am coming to realize that I can't do it alone. My feelings are too strong.

So I decided to call Ron Taffel, a child and family therapist. I figured he'd be sympathetic because when I asked him why it's so hard for parents and teens to communicate, he told me it's because "they live in different worlds."

I also talked to Gretta Mogel, a social worker at the Youth Counseling League in New York City, to see if she could give me any advice.

Because I have never really talked with my parents about things that matter to me, Dr. Taffel suggested that at first I might start by telling them about things going on around me, like how

I feel about problems my friends are dealing with.

For example, I could tell them how I feel about the fact that my friend broke up with her boyfriend, or how I feel about friends who smoke. Eventually, my parents would get used to hearing me talk about how I feel about other people's troubles. And when I'm finally able to tell them my feelings about what is happening to me, they won't be surprised.

Dr. Taffel said I should start small, and then try to work up to talking about the bigger issues.

"It is like comparing trigonometry with basic math," Dr. Taffel said. "If you don't know basic math, how are you going to understand trigonometry?"

Ms. Mogel also suggested I try to make an appointment with my parents, like making a plan to have dinners together on certain nights, so that we can make sure we spend more time together.

Ms. Mogel said that one thing parents should remember when trying to talk to their teens is that they were teenagers at one time and felt the same way we are feeling now.

Start small, and then try to work up to the bigger issues.

And she said teens should remember that usually their parents are not trying to hurt them—they're trying to protect them.

If a teen feels that she can't talk to her parents because her parents don't listen, Ms. Mogel recommended she try writing a letter. It certainly would get the attention of your parents.

Dr. Taffel also told me I was invited to come talk to him if I wanted to, and he suggested that at some point I might want to bring my parents, too.

Now I'm hoping that with the advice I received, I'll be able to take a few small steps to get closer to my parents.

The writer was 16 when she wrote this story. She earned a bachelor's in psychology from City University of New York.

FICTION SPECIAL

Lost and Found

Darcy Wills winced at the loud rap music coming from her sister's room.

My rhymes were rockin'
MC's were droppin'
People shoutin' and hip-hoppin'
Step to me and you'll be inferior
'Cause I'm your lyrical superior.

Darcy went to Grandma's room. The darkened room smelled of lilac perfume, Grandma's favorite, but since her stroke Grandma did not notice it, or much of anything.

"Bye, Grandma," Darcy whispered from the doorway. "I'm going to school now."

Just then, the music from Jamee's room cut off, and Jamee rushed into the hallway.

The teen characters in the Bluford novels, a fiction series by Townsend Press, struggle with many of the same difficult issues as the writers in this book. Here's the first chapter from *Lost and Found*, by Anne Schraff, the first book in the series. In this novel, high school sophomore Darcy contends with the return of her long-absent father, the troubling behavior of her younger sister Jamee, and the beginning of her first relationship.

It's a Family Affair

"Like she even hears you," Jamee said as she passed Darcy. Just two years younger than Darcy, Jamee was in eighth grade, though she looked older.

"It's still nice to talk to her. Sometimes she understands. You want to pretend she's not here or something?"

"She's not," Jamee said, grabbing her backpack.

"Did you study for your math test?" Darcy asked. Mom was an emergency room nurse who worked rotating shifts. Most of the time, Mom was too tired to pay much attention to the girls' schoolwork. So Darcy tried to keep track of Jamee.

"Mind your own business," Jamee snapped.

"You got two D's on your last report card," Darcy scolded. "You wanna flunk?" Darcy did not want to sound like a nagging parent, but Jamee wasn't doing her best. Maybe she couldn't make A's like Darcy, but she could do better.

Jamee stomped out of the apartment, slamming the door behind her. "Mom's trying to get some rest!" Darcy yelled. "Do you have to be so selfish?" But Jamee was already gone, and the apartment was suddenly quiet.

Darcy loved her sister. Once, they had been good friends. But now all Jamee cared about was her new group of rowdy friends. They leaned on cars outside of school and turned up rap music on their boom boxes until the street seemed to tremble like an earthquake. Jamee had even stopped hanging out with her old friend Alisha Wrobel, something she used to do every weekend.

Darcy went back into the living room, where her mother sat in the recliner sipping coffee. "I'll be home at 2:30, Mom," Darcy said. Mom smiled faintly. She was tired, always tired. And lately she was worried too. The hospital where she worked was cutting staff. It seemed each day fewer people were expected to do more work. It was like trying to climb a mountain that keeps getting taller as you go. Mom was forty-four, but just yesterday she said, "I'm like an old car that's run out of warranty, baby. You know what happens then. Old car is ready for the junk heap. Well, maybe that hospital is gonna tell me one of these days—'Mattie Mae Wills, we don't need you anymore. We can get somebody younger and cheaper.'"

"Mom, you're not old at all," Darcy had said, but they were only words, empty words. They could not erase the dark, weary lines from beneath her mother's eyes.

Darcy headed down the street toward Bluford High School. It was not a terrible neighborhood they lived in; it just was not good. Many front yards were not cared for. Debris—fast food wrappers, plastic bags, old newspapers—blew around and piled against fences and curbs. Darcy hated that. Sometimes she and other kids from school spent Saturday mornings cleaning up, but it seemed a losing battle. Now, as she walked, she tried to focus on small spots of beauty along the way. Mrs. Walker's pink and white roses bobbed proudly in the morning breeze. The Hustons' rock garden was carefully designed around a wooden windmill.

As she neared Bluford, Darcy thought about the science project that her biology teacher, Ms. Reed, was assigning. Darcy was doing hers on tidal pools. She was looking forward to visiting a real tidal pool, taking pictures, and doing research. Today, Ms. Reed would be dividing the students into teams of two. Darcy wanted to be paired with her close friend, Brisana Meeks. They were both excellent students, a cut above most kids at Bluford, Darcy thought.

"Today, we are forming project teams so that each student can gain something valuable from the other," Ms. Reed said as Darcy sat at her desk. Ms. Reed was a tall, stately woman who reminded Darcy of the Statue of Liberty. She would have been a perfect model for the statue if Lady Liberty had been a black woman. She never would have been called pretty, but it was possible she might have been called a handsome woman. "For this assignment, each of you will be working with someone you've never worked with before."

Darcy was worried. If she was not teamed with Brisana,

maybe she would be teamed with some really dumb student who would pull her down. Darcy was a little ashamed of herself for thinking that way. Grandma used to say that all flowers are equal, but different. The simple daisy was just as lovely as the prize rose. But still Darcy did not want to be paired with some weak partner who would lower her grade.

"Darcy Wills will be teamed with Tarah Carson," Ms. Reed announced.

Darcy gasped. Not Tarah! Not that big, chunky girl with the brassy voice who squeezed herself into tight skirts and wore lime green or hot pink satin tops and cheap jewelry. Not Tarah who hung out with Cooper Hodden, that loser who was barely hanging on to his football eligibility. Darcy had heard that Cooper had been left back once or twice and even got his driver's license as a sophomore. Darcy's face felt hot with anger. Why was Ms. Reed doing this?

Hakeem Randall, a handsome, shy boy who sat in the back row, was teamed with the class blabbermouth, LaShawn Appleby. Darcy had a secret crush on Hakeem since freshman year. So far she had only shared this with her diary, never with another living soul.

It was almost as though Ms. Reed was playing some devilish game. Darcy glanced at Tarah, who was smiling broadly. Tarah had an enormous smile, and her teeth contrasted harshly with her dark red lipstick. "Great," Darcy muttered under her breath.

Ms. Reed ord e red the teams to meet so they could begin to plan their projects.

As she sat down by Tarah, Darcy was instantly sickened by a syrupy-sweet odor.

She must have doused herself with cheap perfume this morning, Darcy thought.

"Hey, girl," Tarah said. "Well, don't you look down in the mouth. What's got you lookin' that way?"

It was hard for Darcy to meet new people, especially someone like Tarah, a person Aunt Charlotte would call "low class." These were people who were loud and rude. They drank too much, used drugs, got into fights and ruined the neighborhood. They yelled ugly insults at people, even at their friends. Darcy did not actually know that Tarah did anything like this personally, but she seemed like the type who did.

"I just didn't think you'd be interested in tidal pools," Darcy explained.

Tarah slammed her big hand on the desk, making her gold bracelets jangle like ice cubes in a glass, and laughed. Darcy had never heard a mule bray, but she was sure it made exactly the same sound. Then Tarah leaned close and whispered, "Girl, I don't know a tidal pool from a fool. Ms. Reed stuck us together to mess with our heads, you hear what I'm sayin'?"

"Maybe we could switch to other partners," Darcy said nervously.

A big smile spread slowly over Tarah's face. "Nah, I think I'm gonna enjoy this. You're always sittin' here like a princess collecting your A's. Now you gotta work with a regular person, so you better loosen up, girl!"

Darcy felt as if her teeth were glued to her tongue. She fumbled in her bag for her outline of the project. It all seemed like a horrible joke now. She and Tarah Carson standing knee-deep in the muck of a tidal pool!

"Worms live there, don't they?" Tarah asked, twisting a big gold ring on her chubby finger.

"Yeah, I guess," Darcy replied.

"Big green worms," Tarah continued. "So if you get your feet stuck in the bottom of that old tidal pool, and you can't get out, do the worms crawl up your clothes?"

Darcy ignored the remark. "I'd like for us to go there soon, you know, look around."

"My boyfriend, Cooper, he goes down to the ocean all the time. He can take us. He says he's seen these fiddler crabs. They

It's a Family Affair

look like big spiders, and they'll try to bite your toes off. Cooper says so," Tarah said.

"Stop being silly," Darcy shot back. "If you're not even going to be serious . . . "

"You think you're better than me, don't you?" Tarah suddenly growled.

"I never said—" Darcy blurted.

"You don't have to say it, girl. It's in your eyes. You think I'm a low-life and you're something special. Well, I got more friends than you got fingers and toes together. You got no friends, and everybody laughs at you behind your back. Know what the word on you is? Darcy Wills give you the chills."

Just then, the bell rang, and Darcy was glad for the excuse to turn away from Tarah, to hide the hot tears welling in her eyes. She quickly rushed from the classroom, relieved that school was over. Darcy did not think she could bear to sit through another class just now.

Darcy headed down the long street towards home. She did not like Tarah. Maybe it was wrong, but it was true. Still, Tarah's brutal words hurt. Even stupid, awful people might tell you the truth about yourself. And Darcy did not have any real friends, except for Brisana. Maybe the other kids were mocking her behind her back. Darcy was very slender, not as shapely as many of the other girls. She remembered the time when Cooper Hodden was hanging in front of the deli with his friends, and he yelled as Darcy went by, "Hey, is that really a female there? Sure don't look like it. Looks more like an old broomstick with hair." His companions laughed rudely, and Darcy had walked a little faster.

A terrible thought clawed at Darcy. Maybe she was the loser, not Tarah. Tarah was always hanging with a bunch of kids, laughing and joking. She would go down the hall to the lockers and greetings would come from everywhere. "Hey, Tarah!" "What's up, Tar?" "See ya at lunch, girl." When Darcy went to the lockers, there was dead silence.

Darcy usually glanced into stores on her way home from school. She enjoyed looking at the trays of chicken feet and pork ears at the little Asian grocery store. Sometimes she would even steal a glance at the diners sitting by the picture window at the Golden Grill Restaurant. But today she stared straight ahead, her shoulders drooping.

If this had happened last year, she would have gone directly to Grandma's house, a block from where Darcy lived. How many times had Darcy and Jamee run to Grandma's, eaten applesauce cookies, drunk cider, and poured out their troubles to Grandma. Somehow, their problems would always dissolve in the warmth of her love and wisdom. But now Grandma was a frail figure in the corner of their apartment, saying little. And what little she did say made less and less sense.

Darcy was usually the first one home. The minute she got there, Mom left for the hospital to take the 3:00 to 11:00 shift in the ER. By the time Mom finished her paperwork at the hospital, she would be lucky to be home again by midnight. After Mom left, Darcy went to Grandma's room to give her the malted nutrition drink that the doctor ordered her to have three times a day.

"Want to drink your chocolate malt, Grandma?" Darcy asked, pulling up a chair beside Grandma's bed.

Grandma was sitting up, and her eyes were open. "No. I'm not hungry," she said listlessly. She always said that.

"You need to drink your malt, Grandma," Darcy insisted, gently putting the straw between the pinched lips.

Grandma sucked the malt slowly. "Grandma, nobody likes me at school," Darcy said. She did not expect any response. But there was a strange comfort in telling Grandma anyway. "Everybody laughs at me. It's because I'm shy and maybe stuck-up, too, I guess. But I don't mean to be. Stuck-up, I mean. Maybe I'm weird. I could be weird, I guess. I could be like Aunt Charlotte . . ." Tears rolled down Darcy's cheeks. Her heart ached with loneliness. There was nobody to talk to anymore, nobody who had time to listen, nobody who understood.

Grandma blinked and pushed the straw away. Her eyes brightened as they did now and then. "You are a wonderful girl. Everybody knows that," Grandma said in an almost normal voice. It happened like that sometimes. It was like being in the middle of a dark storm and having the clouds part, revealing a patch of clear, sunlit blue. For just a few precious minutes, Grandma was bright-eyed and saying normal things.

"Oh, Grandma, I'm so lonely," Darcy cried, pressing her head against Grandma's small shoulder.

"You were such a beautiful baby," Grandma said, stroking her hair." 'That one is going to shine like the morning star.' That's what I told your Mama. 'That child is going to shine like the morning star.' Tell me, Angelcake, is your daddy home yet?"

Darcy straightened. "Not yet." Her heart pounded so hard, she could feel it thumping in her chest. Darcy's father had not been home in five years.

"Well, tell him to see me when he gets home. I want him to buy you that blue dress you liked in the store window. That's for you, Angelcake. Tell him I've got money. My social security came, you know. I have money for the blue dress," Grandma said, her eyes slipping shut.

Just then, Darcy heard the apartment door slam. Jamee had come home. Now she stood in the hall, her hands belligerently on her hips. "Are you talking to Grandma again?" Jamee demanded.

"She was talking like normal," Darcy said. "Sometimes she does. You know she does."

"That is so stupid," Jamee snapped. "She never says anything right anymore. Not anything!" Jamee's voice trembled.

Darcy got up quickly and set down the can of malted milk. She ran to Jamee and put her arms around her sister. "Jamee, I know you're hurting too."

"Oh, don't be stupid," Jamee protested, but Darcy hugged her more tightly, and in a few seconds Jamee was crying. "She was the best thing in this stupid house," Jamee cried. "Why'd she have to go?"

"She didn't go," Darcy said. "Not really."

"She did! She did!" Jamee sobbed. She struggled free of Darcy, ran to her room, and slammed the door. In a minute, Darcy heard the bone-rattling sound of rap music.

Lost and Found, a Bluford Series™ novel, is reprinted with permission from Townsend Press. Copyright © 2002.

Want to read more? This and other Bluford Series™ novels and paperbacks can be purchased for $1 each at www.townsendpress.com.

Teens:
How to Get More Out of This Book

Self-help: The teens who wrote the stories in this book did so because they hope that telling their stories will help readers who are facing similar challenges. They want you to know that you are not alone, and that taking specific steps can help you manage or overcome very difficult situations. They've done their best to be clear about the actions that worked for them so you can see if they'll work for you.

Writing: You can also use the book to improve your writing skills. Each teen in this book wrote 5-10 drafts of his or her story before it was published. If you read the stories closely you'll see that the teens work to include a beginning, a middle, and an end, and good scenes, description, dialogue, and anecdotes (little stories). To improve your writing, take a look at how these writers construct their stories. Try some of their techniques in your own writing.

Reading: Finally, you'll notice that we include the first chapter from a Bluford Series novel in this book, alongside the true stories by teens. We hope you'll like it enough to continue reading. The more you read, the more you'll strengthen your reading skills. Teens at Youth Communication like the Bluford novels because they explore themes similar to those in their own stories. Your school may already have the Bluford books. If not, you can order them online for only $1.

Resources on the Web

We will occasionally post Think About It questions on our website, www.youthcomm.org, to accompany stories in this and other Youth Communication books. We try out the questions with teens and post the ones they like best. Many teens report that writing answers to those questions in a journal is very helpful.

How to Use This Book in Staff Training

Staff say that reading these stories gives them greater insight into what teens are thinking and feeling, and new strategies for working with them. You can help the staff you work with by using these stories as case studies.

Select one story to read in the group, and ask staff to identify and discuss the main issue facing the teen. There may be disagreement about this, based on the background and experience of staff. That is fine. One point of the exercise is that teens have complex lives and needs. Adults can probably be more effective if they don't focus too narrowly and can see several dimensions of their clients.

Ask staff: What issues or feelings does the story provoke in them? What kind of help do they think the teen wants? What interventions are likely to be most promising? Least effective? Why? How would you build trust with the teen writer? How have other adults failed the teen, and how might that affect his or her willingness to accept help? What other resources would be helpful to this teen, such as peer support, a mentor, counseling, family therapy, etc.

Resources on the Web

From time to time we will post Think About It questions on our website, www.youthcomm.org, to accompany stories in this and other Youth Communication books. We try out the questions with teens and post the ones that they find most effective. We'll also post lesson for some of the stories. Adults can use the questions and lessons in workshops.

> **Discussion Guide**

Teachers and Staff:
How to Use This Book in Groups

When working with teens individually or in groups, using these stories can help young people face difficult issues in a way that feels safe to them. That's because talking about the issues in the stories usually feels safer to teens than talking about those same issues in their own lives. Addressing issues through the stories allows for some personal distance; they hit close to home, but not too close. Talking about them opens up a safe place for reflection. As teens gain confidence talking about the issues in the stories, they usually become more comfortable talking about those issues in their own lives.

Below are general questions that can help you lead discussions about the stories, which help teens and staff reflect on the issues in their own work and lives. In most cases you can read a story and conduct a discussion in one 45-minute session. Teens are usually happy to read the stories aloud, with each teen reading a paragraph or two. (Allow teens to pass if they don't want to read.) It takes 10-15 minutes to read a story straight through. However, it is often more effective to let workshop participants make comments and discuss the story as you go along. The workshop leader may even want to annotate her copy of the story beforehand with key questions.

If teens read the story ahead of time or silently, it's good to break the ice with a few questions that get everyone on the same page: Who is the main character? How old is she? What happened to her? How did she respond? Etc. Another good starting question is: "What stood out for you in the story?" Go around the room and let each person briefly mention one thing.

Then move on to open-ended questions, which encourage participants to think more deeply about what the writers were feeling, the choices they faced, and they actions they took. There are no right or wrong answers to the open-ended questions. Open-ended questions encourage participants to think about how the themes, emotions and choices in the stories relate to their own lives. Here are some examples of open-ended questions that we have found to be effective. You can use variations of these questions with almost any story in this book.

—What main problem or challenge did the writer face?

—What choices did the teen have in trying to deal with the problem?

—Which way of dealing with the problem was most effective for the teen? Why?

—What strengths, skills, or resources did the teen use to address the challenge?

—If you were in the writer's shoes, what would you have done?

—What could adults have done better to help this young person?

—What have you learned by reading this story that you didn't know before?

—What, if anything, will you do differently after reading this story?

—What surprised you in this story?

—Do you have a different view of this issue, or see a different way of dealing with it, after reading this story? Why or why not?

Credits

The stories in this book all appeared in the following Youth Communication publications:

"The Parent Trap," by Lucas Mann, *New Youth Connections*, December 2002

"Finding Our Way Home," by Janelle Allen, *Represent*, January/March/April 2008

"Meeting the Invisible Man," by Athena Karoutsos, *New Youth Connections*, May/June 2005

"Far From the Mom I Love," by Anonymous, *New Youth Connections*, November 2008

"At Home Away From Home," by Odé Manderson, *New Youth Connections*, April 2000

"Prisoner In My Own House," by Anonymous, *New Youth Connections*, January/February 1992

"She'll Always Be My Mother," by Wunika Hicks, *Represent*, March/April 1994

"Mom, Dad, I Have Something to Tell You..." by Jose Jimenez, *New Youth Connections*, May/June 2003

"Not Quite a Family," by Anonymous, *New Youth Connections*, March 1996

"My Father: I Want To Be Everything He's Not," by Troy Shawn Welcome, *New Youth Connections*, May/June 1994

"My Mother Almost Didn't Come Home," by Nicolle Lewis, *New Youth Connections*, March 1995

"He's Not My Grandpa!" by Megan Cohen, *New Youth Connections*, May/June 2005

"Trapped by Mom's Rules," by Anonymous, *New Youth Connections*, May/June 2004

"My Parents Gave Me Everything—Except Themselves," by Lily Mai, *New Youth Connections*, December 2005

"Her Shining Star?" by T. Garrido, *New Youth Connections*, November 2008

"Communication: How to Get It Started," by Anonymous, *New Youth Connections*, April 1998

About Youth Communication

Youth Communication, founded in 1980, is a nonprofit youth development program located in New York City whose mission is to teach writing, journalism, and leadership skills. The teenagers we train become writers for our websites and books and for two print magazines, *New Youth Connections*, a general-interest youth magazine, and *Represent*, a magazine by and for young people in foster care.

Each year, up to 100 young people participate in Youth Communication's school-year and summer journalism workshops where they work under the direction of full-time professional editors. Most are African American, Latino, or Asian, and many are recent immigrants. The opportunity to reach their peers with accurate portrayals of their lives and important self-help information motivates the young writers to create powerful stories.

Our goal is to run a strong youth development program in which teens produce high quality stories that inform and inspire their peers. Doing so requires us to be sensitive to the complicated lives and emotions of the teen participants while also providing an intellectually rigorous experience. We achieve that goal in the writing/teaching/editing relationship, which is the core of our program.

Our teaching and editorial process begins with discussions

between adult editors and the teen staff. In those meetings, the teens and the editors work together to identify the most important issues in the teens' lives and to figure out how those issues can be turned into stories that will resonate with teen readers.

Once story topics are chosen, students begin the process of crafting their stories. For a personal story, that means revisiting events in one's past to understand their significance for the future. For a commentary, it means developing a logical and persuasive point of view. For a reported story, it means gathering information through research and interviews. Students look inward and outward as they try to make sense of their experiences and the world around them and find the points of intersection between personal and social concerns. That process can take a few weeks or a few months. Stories frequently go through ten or more drafts as students work under the guidance of their editors, the way any professional writer does.

Many of the students who walk through our doors have uneven skills, as a result of poor education, living under extremely stressful conditions, or coming from homes where English is a second language. Yet, to complete their stories, students must successfully perform a wide range of activities, including writing and rewriting, reading, discussion, reflection, research, interviewing, and typing. They must work as members of a team and they must accept individual responsibility. They learn to provide constructive criticism, and to accept it. They engage in explorations of truthfulness, fairness, and accuracy. They meet deadlines. They must develop the audacity to believe that they have something important to say and the humility to recognize that saying it well is not a process of instant gratification. Rather, it usually requires a long, hard struggle through many discussions and much rewriting.

It would be impossible to teach these skills and dispositions as separate, disconnected topics, like grammar, ethics, or assertiveness. However, we find that students make rapid progress when they are learning skills in the context of an inquiry that is

About Youth Communication

personally significant to them and that will benefit their peers.

When teens publish their stories—in *New Youth Connections* and *Represent*, on the web, and in other publications—they reach tens of thousands of teen and adult readers. Teachers, counselors, social workers, and other adults circulate the stories to young people in their classes and out-of-school youth programs. Adults tell us that teens in their programs—including many who are ordinarily resistant to reading—clamor for the stories. Teen readers report that the stories give them information they can't get anywhere else, and inspire them to reflect on their lives and open lines of communication with adults.

Writers usually participate in our program for one semester, though some stay much longer. Years later, many of them report that working here was a turning point in their lives—that it helped them acquire the confidence and skills that they needed for success in college and careers. Scores of our graduates have overcome tremendous obstacles to become journalists, writers, and novelists. They include National Book Award finalist Edwidge Danticat, novelist Ernesto Quinonez, writer Veronica Chambers and *New York Times* reporter Rachel Swarns. Hundreds more are working in law, business, and other careers. Many are teachers, principals, and youth workers, and several have started nonprofit youth programs themselves and work as mentors—helping another generation of young people develop their skills and find their voices.

Youth Communication is a nonprofit educational corporation. Contributions are gratefully accepted and are tax deductible to the fullest extent of the law.

To make a contribution, or for information about our publications and programs, including our catalog of over 100 books and curricula for hard-to-reach teens, see www.youthcomm.org

About The Editors

Al Desetta has been an editor of Youth Communication's two teen magazines, *Foster Care Youth United* (now known as *Represent*) and *New Youth Connections*. He was also an instructor in Youth Communication's juvenile prison writing program. In 1991, he became the organization's first director of teacher development, working with high school teachers to help them produce better writers and student publications.

Prior to working at Youth Communication, Desetta directed environmental education projects in New York City public high schools and worked as a reporter.

He has a master's degree in English literature from City College of the City University of New York and a bachelor's degree from the State University of New York at Binghamton, and he was a Revson Fellow at Columbia University for the 1990-91 academic year.

He is the editor of many books, including several other Youth Communication anthologies: *The Heart Knows Something Different: Teenage Voices from the Foster Care System*, *The Struggle to Be Strong*, and *The Courage to Be Yourself*. He is currently a freelance editor.

Keith Hefner co-founded Youth Communication in 1980 and has directed it ever since. He is the recipient of the Luther P. Jackson Education Award from the New York Association of Black Journalists and a MacArthur Fellowship. He was also a Revson Fellow at Columbia University.

Laura Longhine is the editorial director at Youth Communication. She edited *Represent*, Youth Communication's magazine by and for youth in foster care, for three years, and has written for a variety of publications. She has a BA in English from Tufts University and an MS in Journalism from Columbia University.

More Helpful Books From Youth Comunication

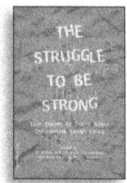
The Struggle to Be Strong: True Stories by Teens About Overcoming Tough Times. Foreword by Veronica Chambers. Help young people identify and build on their own strengths with 30 personal stories about resiliency. (Free Spirit)

Starting With "I": Personal Stories by Teenagers. "Who am I and who do I want to become?" Thirty-five stories examine this question through the lens of race, ethnicity, gender, sexuality, family, and more. Increase this book's value with the free Teacher's Guide, available from youthcomm.org. (Youth Communication)

Real Stories, Real Teens. Inspire teens to read and recognize their strengths with this collection of 26 true stories by teens. The young writers describe how they overcame significant challenges and stayed true to themselves. Also includes the first chapters from three novels in the Bluford Series. (Youth Communication)

The Courage to Be Yourself: True Stories by Teens About Cliques, Conflicts, and Overcoming Peer Pressure. In 26 first-person stories, teens write about their lives with searing honesty. These stories will inspire young readers to reflect on their own lives, work through their problems, and help them discover who they really are. (Free Spirit)

Out With It: Gay and Straight Teens Write About Homosexuality. Break stereotypes and provide support with this unflinching look at gay life from a teen's perspective. With a focus on urban youth, this book also includes several heterosexual teens' transformative experiences with gay peers. (Youth Communication)

Things Get Hectic: Teens Write About the Violence That Surrounds Them. Violence is commonplace in many teens' lives, be it bullying, gangs, dating, or family relationships. Hear the experiences of victims, perpetrators, and witnesses through more than 50 real-world stories. (Youth Communication)

From Dropout to Achiever: Teens Write About School. Help teens overcome the challenges of graduating, which may involve overcoming family problems, bouncing back from a bad semester, or even dropping out for a time. These teens show how they achieve academic success. (Youth Communication)

My Secret Addiction: Teens Write About Cutting. These true accounts of cutting, or self-mutilation, offer a window into the personal and family situations that lead to this secret habit, and show how teens can get the help they need. (Youth Communication)

Sticks and Stones: Teens Write About Bullying. Shed light on bullying, as told from the perspectives of the bully, the victim, and the witness. These stories show why bullying occurs, the harm it causes, and how it might be prevented. (Youth Communication)

Boys to Men: Teens Write About Becoming a Man. The young men in this book write about confronting the challenges of growing up. Their honesty and courage make them role models for teens who are bombarded with contradictory messages about what it means to be a man. (Youth Communication)

Through Thick and Thin: Teens Write About Obesity, Eating Disorders, and Self Image. Help teens who struggle with obesity, eating disorders, and body weight issues. These stories show the pressures teens face when they are confronted by unrealistic standards for physical appearance, and how emotions can affect the way we eat. (Youth Communication)

To order these and other books, go to:
www.youthcomm.org
or call 212-279-0708 x115

www.ingramcontent.com/pod-product-compliance
Lightning Source LLC
Chambersburg PA
CBHW071729090426
42738CB00011B/2423